Cracking the Angels' Code

One Woman's Journey Deciphering
Angelic Messages of What is to Come

Dr. Blinston's Other Written Work:

*When Children Witness the Sacred:
The Lifelong Aftereffects and Disclosure Aspects of
Religious Apparitions Experienced in Childhood*
(https://amzn.to/2t4s36L)

Dr. Blinston as a Contributing Author:

*Fatima Revisited: The Apparition Phenomenon in Ufology,
Psychology, and Science*
(https://amzn.to/2M0wh6k)

Cracking the Angels' Code

One Woman's Journey Deciphering
Angelic Messages of What is to Come

by

Irene Blinston, Ph.D.

Copyright © 2018 Irene Blinston, Ph.D.

All Rights Reserved. No part of this book may be used or reproduced by any means, graphic, electronic, or mechanical, including photocopying, recording, taping, or by any information storage retrieval system without the written permission of the author except in the case of brief quotations embodied in critical articles and reviews.

All maps in this book were obtained from the Library of Congress and are in the public domain.

ISBN-13: 978-1463720117
ISBN-10: 1463720114

Dedicated
to
my mother

Gratitude

Typical with writing a book, there are many people to acknowledge and thank. When I first wrote the gratitude statement for the original manuscript and the second edition, I used everyone's real names. Times have changed, and people have changed, so where I feel it necessary, names have been changed.

First and foremost, I want to thank my mother, Faustina (Tina) Blinston, for being the mother she was. If consciousness does survive physical death, I hope you can hear me, mother. Thank you for nurturing my intuitive abilities. Thank you for your support during the best of times and the worst of times. I hope heaven is all you hoped it would be. I love you.

I also want to thank two of my brothers. To my oldest brother, who often referred to the original manuscript for information from the writings, thank you. When you would share with me what you found, it gave me a sense of validation. To my next to the oldest brother, thank you for reading the first manuscript. Being the only seemingly normal person in the family (you Capricorn, you), it was wonderful you read it through, and had good comments.

To my friends at the time of the original writings, Anne and Helen, thank you. Anne, you recognized my abilities and got me into the world as a professional. Helen, you were a supportive friend and I needed that so much. To my boyfriend at the time, thank you for your patience during the time of my receiving the messages, and the writing of the original manuscript. You were supportive in the face of things you didn't understand. Thank you for still being my friend.

Thank you, Lee and Jan, for being instrumental in the editing of the original manuscript and the printing of the second edition. To all my Facebook friends who helped me choose the best title and the best book cover for this latest and last iteration of this book, you are too many to name, but you know who you are. I love you, thank you!

And, of course, Ankar, Ye, and all the other angels around me, past, present, and future, thank you for sticking with me, and not giving up.

Preface

In the late 1980s, I had encounters with angels. At least, that's what they called themselves. I could not see them in physical form, but they communicated with me.

Over a period of about two years they delivered many messages. Many of the messages were about what is to come, who/what I was in the past, and what we the people on planet earth are now experiencing and the process we are in. They also informed me of my purpose as their messenger and voice.

I wasn't sure I believed what they were telling me or what was happening, but it was in fact happening. I often felt skeptical; yet, I continued to be open to the communication. At the time, I thought I was the only person to whom this was happening. Now, I realize others have also had experiences.

This book is not meant to provide a critical analysis of my experiences, not at all. I have written this book in order to share the experiences I had and the messages I received. It is my intention for you to walk with me through the process I had gone through. I wrote this in the manner I felt would reflect my personality, sense of humor, and inquisitiveness, along with my lingering skepticism. When I realized many of the messages were being validated, my skepticism did wane considerably, but it did not completely disappear.

My view of life had changed as well. As much as I tried to avoid the messages about my mission, the angels did their part in making sure I didn't forget. Each time I attempted to close my eyes and turn my back on it, I would find that as I turned and opened my eyes, there it would be in front of me again in some way, shape, or form.

Even now, as I resurrect this manuscript and edit it as needed, synchronistic signs are making their appearances before me. Admittedly, the first incident did cause my heart to skip a beat, but the subsequent incidences pulled me right back into the investigative mode I was in when the messages first began in 1988. All I can do at this point is shake my head in wonderment. Perhaps these new signs are messages telling me that now is the time to get this book out and re-enter this world of the angels and their messages.

I started the first draft of this manuscript in August 1989. I submitted it to publishers at that time and was rejected by each one. For those publishers who specified the reason for the denial, they indicated that the subject matter was too far out for their company. Seven years later I rewrote the book and tried again. At that time the reason for the rejection was that the topic was too main stream or overdone. I had to laugh. Can't win for losing; or, perhaps it simply wasn't the right time.

Now, I feel a push, if not a bit of an urgency, to get this book out in the world and release it. Not just release it to the world, but to release it from my hold on it and the associated guilt I've felt because of that hold. Fortunately, with print on demand capabilities, I don't have to rely on conventional publishing or expensive self-publishing options. In addition, I can get this book out in the world quickly. Because of this, I have again re-edited and rewritten parts, but not all, of the text. I have kept true to the main content and theme of the original manuscript written in 1989—all angelic communication and my responses to them are from the original. So, without further ado, here is the finished product.

Irene Blinston, Ph.D.
May 20, 2018

P.S. If you have an opinion or thoughts about the content in this book, please share it in a review on Amazon. That way others can benefit.

Table of Contents

Gratitude vii
Preface ix
List of Maps xiii
The Death of My Father 1
Spirit Writing—"Dad, Are You There?" 5
Əfero, the Chosen One 17
Is This My Ego? 29
Fear of Possession 37
Lemuria 45
The New Race—Adam and Eve Revisited 55
The Holocaust 67
The Pact—Your Mission, Should You Choose to Accept It... 73
Revelation, The Angels Are Among Us 87
The Mountain 101
What?! I've Been Here Before?—Plotting Astrology on Maps 109
Validation—Is It True What They Say? 117
My Purpose—Who Am I, And What Am I Doing Here? 123
The End Time, PTSD, and Spiritual Boot Camp 130
What is to Come 138
About the Author 146

List of Maps

Map 1. Lemuria 51

Map 2. Middle East with planetary lines. 112

Map 3. Ankara, Turkey. 113

Map 4. Lemuria with planetary and node lines. 115

Chapter 1

The Death of My Father

When my father died, for some reason that event marked the beginning of my obsessive search for self-improvement. I don't really know why it started then. I suppose I just wanted to be a successful person before I died—successful in something specific and important to me, not anyone else. I wanted to achieve some of my dreams. Life can pass us by so quickly if we let it.

The death of my father raised many questions in me. I questioned life, death, spirituality, and many metaphysical topics. My hunger for knowledge was insatiable. I read book after book. It was not unusual for me to read two and three books at the same time.

I began to expose myself to others thoughts on life, death, and rebirth. Some believe we pick our name, birth date, and parents before incarnating. There is a purpose and objective of some kind. I found this similar to a program on a computer. One knows the capabilities of the program, and where the program will take the user, but it is up to the user to direct it. This is where free will comes into the picture. We are in control of where we direct our destinies. It's an interesting concept but where is the user's manual?

If reincarnation is true, then the vast majority of us are born unfortunate victims of amnesia. There are a few people who claim to remember their past lives, but for the most part, we don't remember why we came back here, or even the fact that we were here before. Sad, but true, we are born strangers in a strange land. Ah, but there's a catch. We left clues to help us find and use our programs. Astrology and numerology are two systems that can help us discover our potentials in this life and give us clues to our past lives as well.

There are some people who seem to have a life direction without any outside help. This direction seems to come from within, either by intuition, or by some other sort of inner guidance. In some spiritual circles, it is said that we have guides who show us the way. Depending on the religion or belief system, these guides can be angels, spirits, both, or something different. These guides may have chosen to be with a particular person, or they may have been appointed, depending on the belief. Some people claim to have seen or talked with their guides, while others think the idea absurd.

Considering the fact that I was raised Catholic, I was led to believe we have guardian angels. Even with eight years of Catholic school and a mother who was a closet occultist, I was never really convinced of anything. As much as I loved occult and supernatural topics, I was still very scientific, and I wanted things proven to me. When answers were not available to my questions, I became frustrated and ultimately claimed myself an atheist when I was eleven years old. As I grew, I tried to maintain a more open mind. Now I tell people I am agnostic. So, with my open mind, I considered the theory of guides interesting. Little did I know, I was soon to discover this theory was very interesting, indeed.

Cracking the Angels' Code

Chapter 2

Spirit Writing—"Dad, Are You There?"

When I was a child, my mother—the closet occultist—taught my brothers and me how to hold a pen to paper and let the spirits of dead people write through us. She called it "spirit writing." Later, I came to discover that this process is also known as automatic writing. My mother and brothers could communicate with the spirits with seeming ease. I would watch their pens move across the paper, quickly forming letters and words. For me on the other hand, it seemed like a practice in futility. Try as I might, that pen would not move.

Every now and then, for some unknown reason, I would insist on putting myself through the frustration of trying to do spirit writing. Early in April of 1988 marked another one of my attempts. There was no one home but me. So, I pulled out a few sheets of paper and my favorite Bic with blue ink, and eagerly sat at the large cherry wood dining room table.

I reasoned, if it's easier to contact someone who was close to me in my life, then my chances were now much better for another shot at it. Since my father was dead, I had a much better chance at success trying to contact him. Besides, there was a huge jackpot in the Wednesday lotto, and who better to contact than a dead gambler with the inside scoop. Yes, I admit it, I was asking for lotto numbers, not ways to promote world peace.

Okay, so it wasn't a real spiritual thing to do. I would like to think I'm a little more spiritually evolved now, but I'm human. It really didn't matter, though. The result of my attempt at spirit writing was the same as it had always been. The pen would not budge. No matter how much I concentrated, no matter how much I tried to visualize my father, that pen stayed in one spot. It was useless, and I was frustrated.

Finally, in my frustration I thought, the heck with it, if anyone wants to say something to me, go for it. To my utter and absolute amazement, the pen began to write. I couldn't believe it. I was really doing it. After all these years, I was actually doing spirit writing. I wanted to call the town crier and let it be known throughout the land. Then I started to wonder, why? After all this time, why did it suddenly start to work now? Did I do something different, or was this my

Spirit Writing—"Dad, Are You There?"

time to receive certain messages of importance? Questions were ringing through my head.

If what I received were messages, I definitely needed an interpreter. I think I'm the only person who writes in tongues. Some of what I had written was in a foreign language, one I didn't recognize. I thought being unable to do spirit writing was frustrating. I never considered being able to do it, and not being able to understand it. However, I didn't give up. It wasn't as though the entire message was foreign, only certain words that seemed to be the main focus. (Oh, great!)

Whoever was writing through me must have thought one word very important, because it was repeated over and over. At first, I thought the word was "O-F-E-R-O." Then I came to find that the first letter was not an "O," but an upside-down "e" ("Əfero"). I was perplexed, and I wanted to learn the meaning and significance of that word. Following is a small excerpt of the writings concerning the word, Əfero.

> Can you repeat what you have to say to me?
> *No.*
>
> Are you angry with me?
> *No, Əfero.*
>
> Is this a message or word that you are supposed to be relaying to me at this time?
> *Yes.*

Will this word cause a radical change in my life as I know it now (April 1988)?
No.

What is the word for?
It is...

It is, what?
It is for you to use.

For me to use in speech, or for the meaning to be used?
The meaning.

How can I find the meaning to this word? Can you tell me?
Yes. (Well?)

Then why don't you tell me?
My purpose is to wake you to the word. It is up to you to find the meaning.

Can you help me find the meaning?
No. (Great, I was obviously going to have to work for this one.)

Can you give me advice on where to look for the meaning?
Yes. You need to look in the dictionary.

What do I look up in the dictionary?

Spirit Writing—"Dad, Are You There?"

Ǝfero.

Well, I looked in the dictionary, and there was no Ǝfero, Efero, Ofero, or anything like it. I thought I had reached a dead end. Because it was not in the dictionary, I had asked if there was another spelling. The reply stated that it was there (in the dictionary), I must look. Keep in mind, at the time I received these writings, there was no Internet, the convenience of Google, or other search engines. Libraries still had card catalogues: long drawers with alphabetized cards in them. Finding information was not as easy as it is today.

After a process not unlike twenty questions, I was able to get a little more to go on. The entity told me that this word came from a language that was the beginning of all languages. Lacking in the necessary education at the time, I presumed that meant Greek or Latin. I later thought that Sanskrit would be a better bet, or even Aramaic. However, the true beginning of all languages is not known, and if it were, I would not have had easy access to it at that time.

I went through the procedure in which I focused on root words. Before I started my search, I thought I'd ask one more time for help. (Okay, I'm a diehard.)

Can you give me the meaning of the word?
Yes. (Hallelujah!)

Can you tell me it's meaning now?
Yes. u-u-u-u-u-u-u-...

Can you tell me its meaning in English, so I can understand?

Yes. You. (Okay, back to the drawing board)

I decided to put this on the back burner for a while and pursue other avenues. I thought it might be nice to know who I was communicating with. I'd been writing all this time and didn't even have a name. So, began my quest for the entity behind the pen.

Am I communicating with my higher self?

No.

Are you an entity with who I should be familiar in this life?

No.

Are you one of my guides?

Yes. (Whoa! Could it be? No way! Irene, remember your open mind? Oh yeah. Okay...well...maybe... I need a break.)

I was so skeptical at the time. Even though I was experiencing the phenomenon, I still didn't fully believe I was being contacted by guides or other types of entities. However, even though I was skeptical, my skepticism didn't stop me from continuing the communication and going deeper into my search for the meaning of that elusive word they were using, "Əfero."

Spirit Writing—"Dad, Are You There?"

This called for an exit to the dictionary to concentrate on "Əfero." A part of me was ecstatic that I had contacted a guide. However, another part of me was questioning the whole thing. I had to keep in mind, I wasn't writing this, at least not consciously. If I wasn't writing it then someone was. Actually, this was quite an achievement for me. Just to have been able to spirit-write at all was really something.

When I again sought the answer to the great mystery, I did not get any further than before, looking through the dictionary in search of "Əfero." I must admit, even though I was frustrated, I was enjoying this adventure.

The next day I decided to pursue the writing and gain more information about my guides. As it was, I had a million questions and had resigned myself to the fact that there really could be guides. On top of that, I had actually contacted one of mine. I decided I would glean all the information I could from my new-found companion. I still didn't know my guide's name. That would be the first line of business; my guide's name.

My guide, are you still there and able to communicate with me?
Yes.

Are you the same guide I talked to yesterday?
Yes.

Do you have a name?
Yes.

What is your name?
Ye.

Are you male or female?
Female.

Are you me? I mean my higher self?
No. eyeeee...

Why are you making continuous e's?
Because it is important to me you-we rewrite everything.

The last answer threw me. I didn't understand what it meant, but I didn't understand a lot of the writing. Maybe later it would all come together, and I could make sense out of it. Besides, I had a new friend in Ye, and I still had a million questions to ask.

My writing continued. It seemed I was stuck for some time trying to find the meaning of "Əfero." As I wrote, I was noticing that Ye kept using the word as if she were addressing me. Could it be? Was she calling me Əfero all this time? On April 16, 1988, this is what was written.

Ye, are you still with me?
Yes, yes Əfero.

Am I Əfero?
Yes.

Are you Əfero?
Yes.

Is Əfero everyone?
Yes. (Confuse me some more)

If Əfero is everyone, is Əfero another name for God?
Yes.

Is Əfero an energy?
Yes.

Then Əfero is the God energy in each of us. Is that correct?
No. (Okay...?)

If Əfero is everyone, and Əfero is another name for God, and Əfero is an energy, then why isn't Əfero the God energy in each of us?
Because God is.

Because God is what?
God. (Yikes! Okay I can handle this. Excuse me while I bang my head against wall.)

I don't know Ye, I guess we'll both have to test our patience. I know it is difficult to try to explain things to me, because I'm lacking in the same comprehension level as you, but let's give it another try. I'm willing, are you?

Yes. I don't want to give up on you. We need you.

Who is we?
We, the others. (There are more?)

I asked questions about the history on Ǝfero, and if anyone knew about the Ǝfero. The reply was that there was a professor of English who was in the Antarctic. He was there to make a discovery of a race of people who lived a million years ago. Then I was told he was dead there, and I would be the one to discover him (uh, I highly doubt that!). Then I asked,

What do you mean?
He is dead, and he is going to be discovered by you in the Antarctic. You will go there to find him, because it is meant to be. He is very important to you. He has all the knowledge you need to continue in your search, your search for enlightenment. You are the one who answers to Ǝfero, and you are the one who is meant to answer to Ǝfero. You are Ǝfero. You must continue your gain of information. You are the chosen one. You are Ǝfero. You are Ǝfero.

What am I meant to do?
You are meant to change the world.

How?
You are meant to change the world.

Spirit Writing—"Dad, Are You There?"

Just me?

No. There are others who will help you in this area of your life. (Well, that's a relief) *You must seek out the mraaaa....*

What is that?

That is the mantra you should use. (Yes, I think this is enough for today. Hmmm... ?)

After my mother finished reading the original manuscript, she informed me that when I was very young (five to seven years old), she overheard me talking while alone in my bedroom. She said I was looking at myself in the mirror. According to my mother, while I was looking at myself in the mirror, I was telling myself that I was going to save the world. She wondered how I could have gotten that idea into my head.

Ironically, one of the areas of research I pursued while in my doctoral program was the use of the psychomanteum, which is a means to contact the deceased. The psychomanteum uses a mirror-gazing technique to bring about an altered state. When in this state, people sometimes experience visions or communication that is believed to come through the mirror. Perhaps when I was a child talking to myself in the mirror, I was actually communicating with "someone" in the mirror or on the "other side" of the mirror. It's an interesting thought to consider.

Cracking the Angels' Code

Chapter 3

Əfero, the Chosen One

As time went on, I began to fall asleep during the writing. This I found very peculiar. I didn't know why I was doing it. I would simply become so tired I found it impossible to keep my eyes open. It didn't matter what time of the day it was, if I wrote, I fell asleep.

Not only was I frustrated by falling asleep, I was starting to become disillusioned, and this frustrated me even more. All of what was being written was so hard for me to believe. I started thinking I was making it all up. Admittedly, a part of me was flattered and excited about what was being written. On the other hand, trying to think logically and realistically, I thought my ego was writing it. Still, even though I questioned it, I continued to write.

My writing continued on a daily basis through April and part of May 1988. For some reason, I can't recall why, I slacked off through June and July. In

August, I began to write again, about once a week. At that time, I began to post the date and time of each of my writings. For some reason, I felt it was important to keep a record. The writing was all done in a 200-page spiral notebook, so everything would be together. It was very much like keeping a journal.

A strange thing happened when I began to write again in August 1988. I found Ye referring to herself as Əfero. Here are a few excerpts of that day.

> Hello, Ye, it's me, are you still with me?
> *Yes.* (The writing is different and unfamiliar)

Who is this?
> *This is Y...* (This seems like Ye, but it has been a while since I've written.)

Who are you?
> *Əfero.*

Okay, who am I?
> *You are...* (The pen made a continuous circular motion.)

What does that mean? (The circular motion)
> *It means everything.* (Okay, let's try again.)

What is your name?
> *My name is Əfero.*

What is my name?

You are Əfero.

If your name is Əfero, and my name is Əfero, then we are the same person. Is that correct?
Yes.

Is my name Əfero too? (Just to clarify)
Yes, we are the same.

I'm getting sleepy. I need to know what you call me. What is my name?
(I'm obviously a little confused.)
Əfero.

Why is my name Əfero?
You are Əfero.

Where did I get this name?
You are Əfero.

Why am I Əfero? Is it from a past life that I got that name?
Yes. (Finally, I'm getting somewhere, and I can't stay awake.)

Can I call you Ye?
Yes.

Well Ye, I will call you Ye, and you can call me Əfero. Is it a deal?
Yes.

Okay, Ye, I was going to ask you a bunch of questions. You probably already know what they were. Anyway, I'm getting too tired to get lengthy on this, but I will ask one question for right now. Do you know what my purpose is in life? You know, what am I supposed to be doing in this life?

> *Everything.* (Great. Well, I wanted to keep it short. I guess it wasn't exactly a simple question, or maybe it was, to Ye.)

Well, this was an interesting turn of events. Ye was me, at least a part of me. No wonder the first time I asked who she was she responded, "Ye." She must have meant Ye, as in you; "I am you."

Is Ye the part of me that remembers the past? Maybe Ye is another entity, but still a part of me. I've read about a theory of parallel lives. Whatever Ye is, she had become my friend and I was glad to have found her. She was always there when I needed someone to talk to. I am grateful for that.

Without a doubt, Ye had filled my life with wonder. It's as if she took me by the hand and was slowly leading me down a path of self-discovery. Each day brought a new adventure. I was beginning to realize that Ye wasn't just words on paper. A personality was behind the words. Ye cared about me, and she wanted to help me. She was my guide. Many times I asked for her guidance, and many times I was surprised at the results.

August 21, 1988 was one of those times. This was the first time Ye had actually written at length. Much of it contained foreign words, most of which I have omitted here.

Guide me, Ye, I need your help.
You are on the road to the me...

Elaborate, Ye.
You are the great, you are the meaning "Əferom"... Əfero me meaning Əfero is "e-r-e-n-i-e"...

What else can you tell me, Ye? (As if I really understood the last answer.)
Əfero, go to the mountain and see another person.

Tell me whatever you think I need to know, Ye.
You are another me. You are Əfero and me. You are another God. You are a special person. You are me and "m-e-a-n-n-o" you are many things. You need to "m" "o-m-e-n" "o-m-e-n." You are meant to be here for man because...

Why?
You are very everything... When you go to see someone, you will know that you are the one.

I am the one?
Yes, you are the chosen one. You are the chosen person to be called upon to let the heal... You are very important to man. You are very important to

everyone. You can be all, you... One day you will come to realize this. You can have all that the world has to offer. You are the one to save all; you are. You can have everything, you can be everything, you are everything.

Why me, Ye?
Because you chose this path before you entered this life.

I chose this before I entered this life?
Yes, you chose to be the savior of this world in the year one thousand and nine. (At first, I thought Ye meant I was supposed to save the world in the year 1009, which would mean I suffered an epic fail on that one. Later I presumed, in the year 1009, I chose to come into this time period and save the world. Hmmm... Right... as if all of this makes sense...)

But this is 1988, not one thousand and nine.
Yes, but that is the time you chose. You came here to be everything you could be.

But, Ye, isn't that true of everyone? I mean all people.
Yes.

Then, Ye, why do you say I am the chosen one?

Əfero, the Chosen One

Because you are. You are going to be chosen by all people to be a leader. Every time you question me. You are meant... Every time you are letting me tell you things you don't want to hear. Aren't you ready for this?

You tell me.

You are ready. You have to be ready. You can't go out there with doubt in your mind.

Why?

You have to be strong. You have to have strength to fight those who are bad, those who are out to hurt man. You are the person. You chose this, Əfero. You chose to do this job.

When will I know it's begun?

It has begun. You are needed now by many. You are needed today.

Ye, this is really hard for me to believe. What am I supposed to do?

You must go to the mountain and see a man. See a man named "Eveani" and make him "l-e-n-e-n-m"... You must go. You are the one.

Are they expecting me?

No, they don't know about you yet.

When am I supposed to go?

You must go when you know the time is right. You must be ready.

What is the name of the man I see?
His name is another name that you know.

What does that mean?
You must go feed the dogs. (What? That's a good way of getting out of telling me.)

Okay, Ye, but please tell me the name of the man I'm supposed to see on the mountain.
His name is Anemem, and you will see another, and each one will help you on your way. We love you. You are the one, please m-e-a-n-n-a-n-a-d, you are the one. New one of your friends will help you. Every time you can think of it, please ask, and you shall receive.

Who is the man on the mountain, and what is he to me?
He is a soul who you know from the past. A longtime ago he was there when you were born. He has a lot to do with your life now. You don't realize it, but he is your soulmate. He is your God. He is your life. You are from a long time ago. You are from a place far away. You are the chosen one. You are the one who many depend on. Please mean the things you say. Never lie to them. You are the one. Can you mean

Ə̵fero, the Chosen One

what you say? You have got to make the change. You have got to make the changes for a life of many happinesses for everyone. A long time ago you chose to be the one. You chose to be Ə̵fero. You chose to be Irene. You chose to be with us. You are the chosen one... Am..."m-e-i-n-m-e-a-n...

This is so hard for me to believe. I really feel like my ego is getting in on this. I really feel like my ego is making all this up!

No, it is not your ego. It is the way it is. It is the way you chose when you came... Ə̵fero.

Okay, how will I know I'm ready?

You will know. You are ready now, you can go now. When you are ready in your heart, you will go. You have much to learn.

What do I need to learn?

You must learn humility. You must learn to be patient with yourself and others. Let go of fear. ...one, you are Ə̵fero. You are the one. You are Ə̵fero.

Am I speaking to more than one of you?

No. We are all one. We are all you. (Okay, this is interesting and a bit mind-blowing)

Who is "we"?

We are you. You are us.

Are you my guides?

No. We are you.

Do I have guides?
Yes, they are with you now. They are always looking after you. They are your special guides. They are with you always. They were chosen by you when you chose this life. You are the...

Was Әfero the name given me at birth?
No. It was given to you when all came to the temple. You were anointed with oil and given the new name "Әfero."

What about my sister? (Әfero had an older sister, Gentrana. This was written to me earlier, but I had omitted it until now.)
She was born as Gentrana and remained Gentrana.

What does Әfero mean? (I never give up.)
Әfero means everything, everything.

What was my birth name?
You were given a name not mentioned after you were anointed Әfero.

In other writings, you mentioned there were other anointed ones.
Yes, they are all of whom you know.

What was the significance of being anointed?
You must be an anointed one to be of the temple.

Ɵfero, the Chosen One

Was it known when I was born that I was the chosen one?

Yes, it was. You were a gift to the world. You were sent from heaven by a group of angels, you were a gift to the world.

Who was my mother?

You were without a mother. You were from heaven. You were sent by God. You see when Gentrana was born she prepared the way for you. God had sent a savior; God sent Ɵfero.

What happened? Did I suddenly materialize? I had to be born or something.

No. You were brought from heaven an infant, and you were laid in the arms of your Earth mother. She was chosen for you by God. (Gentrana, on the other hand, was born the old-fashioned way.)

Chapter 4

Is This My Ego?

My skepticism was becoming greater. I was almost sure it was my ego doing the writing. To make it worse, a part of me was feeding off of this. I was flattered and excited. Without a doubt that was my ego. I knew I needed to talk to someone with knowledge of metaphysics and psychology. I needed someone I didn't know well, someone unbiased and objective.

A year or so earlier, a friend of mine, Anne, took me with her to a class taught by a prominent psychic and metaphysician from the San Francisco Bay Area. Her name was Michelle. Anne introduced me to her. Once a week Michelle would come to Sacramento to teach and see clients. She worked out of the home of one of her associates named Helen, an upcoming psychic in the Sacramento area. I had seen Helen's picture in a magazine put out by a large metaphysical bookstore. I felt I needed to meet her. I felt compelled to introduce myself.

The metaphysical bookstore had a monthly psychic fair in which Helen participated. I went to the fair and purchased a reading from Helen. This was the only way I knew I could meet her and talk to her. I didn't see Helen again for almost a year from that first reading. It was Michelle's birthday and Anne brought me along to meet with Michelle and Helen at a Sacramento restaurant. The meeting was short and Helen didn't remember me, but she assured me she wouldn't forget me again, and so she didn't.

Two months later, in August, we met at another psychic fair, and we were becoming good friends. At the time, I never associated this new friend, to the "new one of your friends will help you," mentioned in my writings.

Michelle was well schooled. She had degrees from a school of metaphysics in San Francisco. She had the knowledge and ability to help me. We weren't close enough to cause her opinion to be biased or subjective. She was perfect.

In the latter part of September 1988, I went to see Michelle, and I talked about my writings. She assured me it wasn't my ego. I felt better, but I must admit, I still wasn't sure. I felt if Ye wrote to Michelle, the essence of Ye would be in the paper. Michelle could use psychometry (the ability to obtain information from an object being held in the reader's hand), and feel the energy, maybe even pick up some images. This would help Michelle form a more precise opinion. I decided it was worth a try, so I did it. I discovered interesting new things from those writings.

I was told that the time of Ɵfero was "the time that it all began with you, and that is when it will all begin again." I was also told a little more about the life and times of Ɵfero. I was told there was a "Temple of Ankar." There was a priestess there, who was the daughter of "the great winged angel, Ananda." At the time of the writings, I had never before heard of this word, Ananda. It was several years later that I learned "ananda" is a Sanskrit word meaning "bliss."

Ye wrote directly to Michelle.

Yes, Michelle, it has been a longtime. You are always in my heart. You are always a part of me. There is much to do. There is much to accomplish in this short time. Can you remember all the times we were together? Can you remember the time we went all the way to the ancient temple and found our brother across the river? He had many answers to all our questions. Can you remember when we were together with another group of soldiers on our way to battle, and we stopped to pray, and all the others prayed with us? Do you remember me?

My name is Ankar. My name is Ankar.

I immediately thought to myself, who is Ankar? Could it be I had another guide? Maybe he just came through for Michelle and he had nothing to do with me. Regardless, I found this very interesting and it had me pondering the implications of having more than one guide.

To the surprise of us all, there actually was a "great winged angel" seen watching over Michelle. Helen had seen it. This incident took place long before Ye wrote to Michelle. I was told about it when I called Helen to see what Michelle's reaction was to the writings I sent her. This marked the first time, of many, that proved my writings to be true. This was a bit of a shock to me. I thought, if this was true, is all that has been written about me true? If I am the chosen one, just how am I supposed to go about saving the world? Seriously.

Ye wrote about the people, and how they need help. Ye wrote of the "anglomen" or "anglomenen." She informed me "they were a part of what was, and still are." She told me I had forgotten about them, but they are still out there.

Ye wrote,

> *Can you see that? Can you see what is going on in the world? It's all about the angry people, the greedy people, about the bad people and more.*

What was I supposed to do? How could I make a difference? Most of the time I tried to put it out of my mind. I would continue to write, hoping the answers would come.

On October 11, 1988, Ankar began to write. I could tell because the "feeling" was different. It's as though I could feel Ye and know it's her. This time, when the pen moved, I knew it wasn't Ye. Someone different was writing, so I asked who it was.

Who is this?
This is Ankar. (Somehow, I knew Ankar was male)

Who are you Ankar?
I am the one. (He drew a strange symbol.) *...help him, he is already here. You are my helper. You are my helper on this plane. You are the way. You are the way and the glory. You are the one. You are the chosen one. You are the chosen one, and you...help them... meaning all are men...* (He begins to make a continuous circle.) *Ǝfero my friend and helper.*

He wrote about an aboriginal person during the time of Ǝfero. I asked about this person.

Who was he to Ǝfero?
He was your guardian. He was here to protect you.

Why was he my guardian?
Because he was chosen among several for the job.

Who hired him?

> *He and others were hired by your father. The Andreanar were a tribe of people, and they were without names. You were in love with him, but your father would allow no announcement of this because it was not accepted; it was taboo.* (This is starting to sound like a romance novel) *You see, you were an anointed one. You were a special child. You were Əfero, the chosen one. You were here to save the world, and no one could approach you. You were sacred, you were like an idol. You were like a living god.* (Oh brother, you've got to be kidding)

Who is writing this?
> *Ankar and Ye and You. Yes, we are the same and we are all different. It really does make sense.* (Okay, if you say so.)

This is all so intriguing. Life is such a mystery. No one really knows what life is, or what death is, but the variety of thought on the subject makes for interesting study. With the knowledge I now possess, I realize what Ankar wrote that day does make sense to a degree. However, at the time of the writings, what he wrote made no sense to me at all. I was often quite confounded.

I questioned the concept of reincarnation. The topic is so complex. It seems that every religion has its own belief. Where do they come up with this direction or thought? I can understand the thinking of the newer religions, as it is usually a revised or equal form of an already established view. It's the older and ancient religions that baffle me. What vision. What brilliant minds were had by those philosophers from the past.

Whether their thoughts be true or not, it makes no difference. These people will be remembered. These special people with seeming second sight, made their thoughts known. Because of this, they will remain immortal. Abraham, Mohammed, Buddha, Jesus, to name a few, will be remembered and revered. They are considered divine prophets.

This makes me wonder how Ankar came to be known by Ǝfero and her people. Was he a divine prophet? Was he a god of that time? Why did he have his own temple?

Why was Ǝfero looked upon as an "idol" and a "living god"? Perhaps it was similar to the Jewish belief in the "messiah." Could it be, for some reason, Ǝfero's people thought she was their prophesied "messiah"? I had an endless list of questions.

Chapter 5

Fear of Possession

One day while visiting with my friend, Anne, I was asked to do some writing for her. She had some questions she wanted to ask Ye. I obliged her and wrote. The few questions she had to ask quickly turned into to several questions. I sat and wrote for at least an hour.

Within the writings a story began to unfold about Əfero's life and family. Pieces were revealed about the temple and the high priestess. We were informed that the high priestess and her apprentice were cousins to Əfero. Ye told us that, during the time of the temple, there was much jealousy and tension on their part toward Əfero. The whole story was quite fascinating.

In my mind's eye, I could actually see the whole picture of what was being conveyed. It was as if I was there, actually watching and feeling these things happening. When Ankar wrote to Michelle about the soldiers praying, I could see many weary men dressed in the uniforms of the crusades. There were two men off by themselves, kneeling and praying with their heads bowed. I could feel the true faith these men felt. There was also an underlying fear they felt, concerning the uncertainty of their futures.

Whenever Ye writes about the high priestess, I see a young woman in her late twenties or early thirties. She has hip length, wavy ash blonde hair. She's wearing a white gown with rope-like ties that cross over the chest and wrap around the waist. The garment is very similar to those in which angels are depicted.

I couldn't see her face. Her back was turned to me. She was facing a large stone altar in what appeared to be underground or in a cave. The images I received during the writings magnified my interest in the information. It was like watching, or even being part of, a great epic movie.

When I finished writing for Anne that day, she decided to send the writings to Michelle. Anne thought Michelle could do psychometry on the papers and receive some impressions. Perhaps the writings could give Michelle another item to work with, particularly in case the energy varied.

A few days later I received a phone call from Anne. She had heard from Michelle and was very concerned. The use of spirit writing and Ouija Boards was a means of connecting with low energy entities. If one was susceptible, one could become possessed by these entities. Anne asked me to stop doing the writing. She wanted me to cleanse my house and banish everyone (entities and spirits).

I must confess, what Anne told me scared me. She had hit a sensitive nerve when she mentioned possession. I had seen the movie, "the Exorcist." Okay, I admit it; I didn't see the whole movie. I kept my eyes closed through most of it—but believe me, it was still very effective. It was after watching that movie that I proclaimed myself agnostic instead of atheist. I came to the conclusion there is just as much probability as not that there is a God. So, what the heck, I would stay neutral. I have no set or firm beliefs. I open myself up to all beliefs and all possibilities.

I went through my house with frankincense to cleanse it. Then I went through a banishing routine I had read in a few books. Cleansing the house wasn't hard but banishing Ye was devastating. The thought of it broke my heart. I talked to her first. I told Ye and Ankar, that if they were really here for my highest good, they would stay outside of my set perimeters. This was at least until I was sure or had more confidence in what was going on. I apologized to them and hoped they would understand. I knew they did understand and would respect my feelings. I put away my spiral notebook, and I didn't use it for anything else. I couldn't bring myself to get rid of the writings. Their value to me was still too great.

After that day, my life felt empty. I felt I'd lost my best friend. My heart was broken. The only consolation I had was that I knew Ye and Ankar were still there. I could feel them around me, but they kept their distance. I felt their protective and watchful eyes over me all the time. At least I had the comfort of knowing they hadn't given up on me. They were sticking with me no matter what. For that I was grateful.

From the time the writings started, I had never felt anything of a negative nature emanating from them. I was convinced they were only good. The fear of possession had come over me, and from that time my judgment was clouded. A somewhat humorous part to this is the fact that I wasn't sure if I even believed in possession, but why take chances, you know?

During the last weekend in October 1988, I worked my first large psychic fair as a reader. I was reading numerology and runes. I had discovered the runes and felt an immediate connection to them. I started that morning thinking I would be the only new person. I found myself to be mistaken in that thinking. There were several new people working that show, and one was my neighbor in the booth to my right. She was a direct psychic and did psychometry. We introduced ourselves and shook hands.

When she shook my hand, a look came over her face. It can only be described as amazement with reverence. She looked down at our clasped hands, and then looked up at my face. I'll never forget, with her eyes wide she said, "Oh. You're so holy." One can imagine my surprise. If she hadn't been an unknown person and looked so amazed, I would have believed someone paid her to say that!

I wondered if she had somehow known about my writings. She couldn't have known. She didn't even know me. She didn't know anyone who knew me or any of the writings. I felt I had to tell her about Ye and Ankar and what was written. I didn't go into detail. I told her only a small amount. I spent the majority of the conversation focusing on the fact that I had banished them. I conveyed to her how much I had missed Ankar and Ye. She advised me to go with what I felt inside. If I felt they were positive, then I should go with that feeling and continue to write. Helen, who was also working the show, confirmed what the woman said.

Helen brought up the subject of the "light." She told me all entities are supposed to answer whether they are or are not of the light. The "light" I presumed was what they considered "God Light." All I need do was ask if Ankar and Ye were of the light. It sounded simple enough. I couldn't wait to get home and dig out my faithful spiral notebook. So, I did.

October 31, 1988 (9:20am PST)
Ye, are you here with me?
Yes, I am.

Ye, are you of the light?

Yes, I am. You are also of the light.

Ye, I have missed you. (I wanted to cry.)
Yes, I have missed you too. You are all that is. You are all that is.

Who are you?
I am Ye. (I felt a need to be sure it was Ye writing. Even though I knew the feel of the pen, I still had fear of negative energy.)

Who am I?
You are Ɵfero. You are not sure about me. You are not sure if I am of the light. You are afraid of me, if I am a "neetna," an evil one, and you are afraid that I will misguide you. Also, you are afraid that you will become possessed. You will not. You see, we already are one. We already are one.

This statement of Ye's, "We already are one," intrigues me to this day, from a spiritual perspective and from a psychological perspective.

What are you to me, Ye?
You are to me, to me. You are to me an angel of heaven. You are here for a special person [purpose?]. *You are here to help those in need. You are to me. You are to me.*

Why are you with me, Ye?

I am with you because you need guidance, and I am here to guide you through all the evil areas you may enter. You see you will be trekking [through] many areas of danger. You are going to trek in many areas of danger, and I will help you. This is Ye, my angel. You are safe with me. You are safe with me. You need much guidance. You need much guidance. You are going to face much opposition. You need to be with many good souls.

Who are these "good souls"?
You will meet them and they will let you know.

Obviously, this was going to have to be a waiting game, and one of trust. I didn't ask everyone I met if they were good souls, but for a time I did observe people with more diligence and discernment.

Chapter 6

Lemuria

The same day I started to write again, I asked Ye and Ankar to write to my friend, Helen. From this I learned a little more about the life of Əfero, and Helen learned about her connection to that life.

October 31, 1988 (9:24 am PST)
Ye, would you say something to Helen?
Yes. I am Ye. I am the protector of Əfero. Never cross her for she will depend on you. You are here for her as well. You are here to help her. You chose to do this for her. You are a special angel as well. You need to go to the mountain with Əfero. You need to take her there, and you can see him, you can see the ancient one there. (I had so much fear around going anywhere that could possibly validate what was being written, I wasn't acting on what I was being told. They evidently thought it would make a difference if Helen were to take me to

the mountain, but they were wrong. At that time, I still wouldn't go.)

What mountain, Ye?
The mountain that has the angel and the mountain that has the caves. It will not be easy, it will not be easy. You see you are an angel, and you are an angel of ages. You are an angel of ages. You will know all very soon. You will know all.

What about Helen, Ye?
She is meant to go with you. She is meant to go with you. (I could tell this was not Ye writing.)

Who is this?
This is Ankar.

Who are you, Ankar? (I finally ask)
I am the angel of the temple. I am Ankar. I am Ankar. You are Ɵfero. You are the chosen one. You are a special angel. You are a special angel. You are a... (I cut him off)

Are you and Ye the same beings or entities?
Yes and no. You see we are all an energy of you.

Are you of the light? (this question was long overdue.)
Yes, we are... You have got to start trusting your own feelings.

Why is Helen so familiar to me?
She was with you in the temple. She was with you at the time of the great escape from the holocaust. It was a very sad time. You were so young.

I always thought of the Jewish holocaust when hearing that word. I looked it up and was somewhat surprised at what I discovered. Holocaust also means complete destruction by fire, even a sacrifice by fire.

I continued questioning Ankar regarding Helen.

Who was she to me, and how old were we?
She was your sister, and she was your best friend. She was always with you. She was the only one allowed to touch you. She was your best friend. She was your "gandana"(?). She was also jealous of you, because you were the chosen one and not her, but she still loved you very much.

Who is this writing?
This is Ankar and Ye, and all who watch over you. Everyone loves you, Ɵfero, and we are all here to protect you. We love you. We love you.

What was Helen's name then?
It was Gentrana. It was Gentrana, she was your sister. She was another of the temple. She was older than you. She was at the age of eleven years. You were at the age of ten. You were separated at that time, and you were sent to the temple. Gentrana was

sent away and only allowed to see you on special holidays. She was very sad for you, because you would cry all the time. You were so lonely for your sister and friend.

What happened to us?
You stayed at the temple. Gentrana also worked at the temple with the high priestess.

What did she do at the temple?
She was there to carry all the necessary tools for the high priestess. She was the apprentice for her.

What about me (Ɵfero)?
You were locked away. You were not seen except on special holy days. You were not allowed to be touched by anyone, not anyone except your sister Gentrana. She was the only one. Not even the high priestess could desecrate you by a touch. You were a sacred child. You were the chosen one.

Where were we, Ye?
You were in an area now called ancient Lemuria. You were on the hidden continent. You were the last ones to stay. You perished there with many others.

This was all unbelievable. I figured, true or not, this was the greatest story, and now Lemuria was brought into the picture. I had always been familiar with the myths and legends of Atlantis, but I had never heard of Lemuria. You can imagine my dismay when I looked in the dictionary to discover there was actually a Lemuria mentioned. Thus, began another mad search for information. It didn't take me long to see there wasn't a great deal written on the subject. If there were more books about Lemuria available during the time I was receiving the messages, I didn't know where to find them.

Within a day or two after Ye wrote about Lemuria, I received a phone call from my oldest brother. He lived in the Los Angeles area. He would call me periodically to discuss the different books that he had found. How "coincidental" it was when he told me about the book he had just purchased. The book was about the first races of people and the four original continents, one of which was Lemuria. He talked about the holocaust that caused the destruction of the four continents. According to the author of that book, this incident was so severe it caused a polar shift to the Earth.

All the time I was writing, I never told my family. In fact, only a handful of people knew about it. I guess I thought it was a lot of fun, and interesting, but no big deal. At least I didn't want to believe it was a big deal. I didn't want to believe all the messages I was receiving were true. After hearing what my brother was reading, I was beginning to see a definite possibility for just that—the messages may in fact be true. This made me somewhat uncomfortable. I couldn't believe my ears.

Did he just say "holocaust"? I tried to tell my brother what I was doing. I tried to tell him about my writings and Lemuria. For some reason, I don't think it completely sunk in.

He was so enthralled in his new book, it definitely took precedence over my writings. It didn't matter. The only thing I cared about at the moment was that another one of my writings had been validated. I was in shock. I kept wondering, what could this all mean? Why am I writing this stuff?

In an article I read, there was mention of Lemuria. It was stated, Lemuria was believed to be an Island continent south of the Middle East, between India and Africa. The article was about "Lemurs," a small tree dwelling primate indigenous to the tropical areas of India, Africa, and Madagascar. The article mentioned a theory or legend in which is believed the lemur was only found in Lemuria, much like the Koala in Australia. It was believed when Lemuria sank, the lemurs swam for the nearest land, thus placing them where they are now.

Another interesting tidbit I read about gave more evidence of the possibility of Lemuria. The very small islands in the Indian Ocean are of a type called continental, as opposed to volcanic or otherwise. This means the islands are believed to be part of a continent, instead of built up by volcanic action, such as the Hawaiian Islands. Therefore, these islands would have had to be a part of Africa, or a continent that, for whatever reason, is no longer in existence. If these islands were not a part of Africa, then they must have been a part of another land mass. Could that land mass have been Lemuria? Perhaps the islands are the high mountain peaks of a submerged island continent. This certainly creates food for thought.

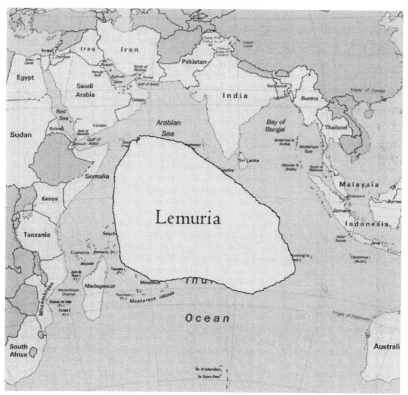

Map 1. Lemuria

I found this information about Lemuria and the islands very interesting, because it fit with the images I received in my mind. When communicating with

Ankar and Ye about Lemuria, my visions put me on a land mass in the Indian Ocean.

In addition, I felt there must have been a trade connection with what is now Turkey, because Turkey was prominent in my feelings. The country seemed like it would be quite a trek for Lemurians, but I just knew there was a connection to Turkey.

You can imagine my utter shock and surprise when I discovered that "Ankara" was the capital of Turkey. What a synchronicity that city name was practically the same name as an entity that had been communicating with me! I was a bit dumbfounded, but I began to wonder if I might find the meaning of the word, Əfero, in the Turkish language. That led me on a search and study of additional foreign languages, but I was unsuccessful in my search.

When one thinks back, Turkey and the Middle East were once all part of Persia. Those lands that made up Persia had coastlines on the Mediterranean Sea and the Indian Ocean. This made those seaports accessible to Lemurian ships, if indeed, Lemuria was actually there. My visions and thoughts led me to believe that Lemuria was, in fact, those lands that made up Persia (Turkey and the Middle East). It also could be, if there was an island, it was part of Lemuria, much like Sicily and Sardinia are part of Italy.

I have another interesting point fitting with my Persian territory theory. Remnants and remains found from what is to be the oldest civilization unearthed so far, were dug up between the Tigris and Euphrates rivers. The area was called Mesopotamia. This area extends from the southern part of Turkey through Syria and Iraq. These three countries were all part of Persia. When one envisions the aforementioned countries, one sees hot deserts and an arid climate. It was different in the Mesopotamian Valley. The ground was fertile and the climate was conducive to farming. There were no extremes in the weather, which made for comfortable living year-round.

My theory does contain flaws. The artifacts found in the Mesopotamian Valley were those of the Sumerians. A people extinct since about 3000 B.C. The tablets found there date back to 4000 B.C. When I asked about the time of Əfero's life, Ye wrote, "About thirteen thousand years before Jesus was born." This leaves nine thousand years before the Sumerians. Nine thousand years is quite a lengthy period of time. Certainly, there has been evidence found of people existing long before the Sumerians, but those were not ancient civilizations (that we know of).

If Lemuria was in the Indian Ocean, it had a tropical climate, if the weather was as it is today. When the island was destroyed, perhaps there were those who made an escape. Possibly there were different groups of people who made it to surrounding land masses. A group could have made it to the Persian Gulf, continuing up until they found a place suitable to settle. As they continued up the Gulf they may have eventually reached the mouth of the Tigris River. After traveling up the river they may have found the perfect place for their new home. Perhaps the surviving Lemurians were the ancestors to the Sumerians. No one really knows, but it is definitely an interesting idea to consider

Chapter 7

The New Race—Adam and Eve Revisited

The people of Lemuria were of a race that I can only presume were similar to those who currently inhabit the Middle East. During the time of Əfero, a change was taking place in the people. I was told by Ankar and Ye, God had given a gift to the world. He had given the beginning of a new race; a race of superior beings. I asked several questions concerning this.

I'm baaaaack... (I have to keep it light or I'd go crazy.)

Yes, we know. You are such a character sometimes, and we love you.

As you know, I have a million questions to ask. Let's start with, who were Əfero's parents and what were they at that time?

Your parents were of great nobility. They were of great and noble angelican.

What does that mean?
They were angelican. They were of the angels. They were of the angels.

What did they do in Lemuria?
They were the rulers of the land of the angels. All the Earth was a land of angels. There were those of human form as well. You and Gentrana were of the angels. You were of angelic birth. You see, at the time, the Earth was the home of the angels. That is when you came.

Came from where?
You would call it heaven, but heaven is in your universe. It is in the galaxy of stars outside this solar system. You came to Earth many eons ago and lived among the people here. They were as we see in books; the primitive people. They were of the land. You were of the heavens.

All of the anointed ones were of the heavens?
Yes, you were all angelican, and you were considered sacred by the people. You were of the winged angels, and the people of the Earth thought you were half bird and half human. You were in fact from a

The New Race—Adam and Eve Revisited

different world, and you were closer to God, that's all. You knew God and they were learning.

What about the aboriginal people (from Australia)?

They were from another world as well. They were here when the angelics arrived. They had been here for a long time before.

What was Əfero's [adoptive] mother's name? Was she born here or in heaven?

Her name was Krantana, and she was born on this planet.

What about Əfero's [adoptive] father?

His name was Adama, and he was of the heavens. He was the ruler of the land. He, like Əfero, came from the heavens. You were gifts from the heavens. He was here as a young child and grew-up with a noble family. You see, all is not as you had suspected. You were not aware that the angels came to live on the Earth. They were all destroyed or left to escape the destruction, and they all went home. Can you understand that?

Well, I must say this was news to me. I found it more and more difficult to accept this as real, if I were anywhere near accepting it in the first place. At the time, I thought Ankar's use of the name "Adama" a convenient response. Yet, I later discovered there has been reference to a being/entity known as "Adama," who is associated with the Lemurians and with Mount Shasta, here in Northern California. Needless to say, I was quite shocked to discover this detail. This was yet another validation of the messages I received.

Ankar and Ye kept referring to "God," and I am opposed to that word, if not the Christian concept of some old guy who wields a mighty temper. It did make me wonder, if I was supposed to be this little angel, then how could I be an agnostic in this life? I did not let that stop me, though. This story was much too captivating to stop writing about, and I continued to ask questions. I did maintain a sense of humor through it, and they tolerated me.

As I work through this book now, I can't help but wonder about Ye and Ankar's statement, "You were in fact from a different world, and you were closer to God, that's all. You knew God and they were learning." When they conveyed that the earth people didn't know God but were learning, I had this uncomfortable feeling as if entities from another world came to this planet to proselytize their god, not unlike the Christians forcing their religion on the Indigenous Americans as well as the Hawaiians, Japanese, Filipinos, and other Island folk they happened upon in their sea travels. I hope this wasn't the case for the angels, and they were tolerant of all the inhabitants' spiritual beliefs or lack thereof.

The New Race—Adam and Eve Revisited

As I continued to ask Ankar and Ye about the angels living on Earth, they continued to explain what life was like then. It was relayed to me that there were volunteers among the angels. There was some plan to create a special race of people who were half human and half angel. This new race was very special. Angels volunteered to be part of this "project." They came and mixed with the humans and bore children of the "new race." This was their job. Actually, I feel if this was true, they came here to live, love (I hope), and marry among the inhabitants of Earth.

It was also appearing in the writings that there may have been at least two types of angels. There was mention of the "winged angels" and just angels. Ye wrote about one of the female angels that came to earth. Her name was Ananda. Ye wrote, "Ananda fell in love with a beautiful and wise angel of earth. That is to say a human being, not a winged angel." Perhaps there was a difference.

Ye went on to write:

She was here to give birth and have special children of human blood. All angels and humans were of a very special type. The combination created a very special offspring. She, Ananda, was a very sacred angel. She and her sister came and had interaction with humans, and thus created children for the earth. You and Gentrana were of angelic birth. That is why you were so sacred. You were of the heavens. You were all gifts from God. You were all the special reward of the people, and after Ǝfero had come, much peace had come over the land. Lemuria was a peaceful existence. Another area of the earth was of a hostile nature, and thus set out to take the world as their own.

Did Gentrana and I have wings? (I couldn't help myself, I just had to ask.)

Yes, but they were not used. They were taken off by the angels of heaven, and you were left without them on the earth. (Humor Alert: Helen figured they removed the wings because it was hard for the fashion-conscious angel to find up to date styles that fit. It made sense to me. *wink*)

I am very much on the fence concerning angels and their wings. Ancient artifacts show winged beings, but are they only metaphoric depictions of the particular power or abilities of the beings? I do not have the specific education or any degree of study in this area to know enough to discuss the topic. However, I do find the subject matter interesting, especially in the context of these writings. I asked Ye why she was pushing the life of Ǝfero.

What is its significance now?

You have the opportunity in this life to take advantage of this knowledge. You can now help the people from being massacred again. You have the ability. You are here for this chance. You have waited and lived for thousands of years, to be able to make the earth another angelic planet; another heaven. Is this all starting to make sense now? (Not really... well, maybe...) *We have a chance to begin again. We have a chance to make Lemuria a thing of the present. All of you know why you are here. We, of the angels, are here to bring about a change, in hopes of saving the world before it is too late, and all is lost forever.*

This was like reading about "Adam and Eve, The Remake." I especially loved the part about heaven being a planet in another galaxy. This was too bizarre. This went against all I was taught at good ol' St. Thomas School. This stuff would give Sister Cordelia a coronary.

Attempting to maintain an open mind, I remained accepting and without judgment. Besides, how do we really know anything to the contrary? Nothing has been proven either way. Until such a time there is proof, I'll remain open and unswayed.

In most Christian belief, following the Bible, Adam and Eve were the first humans, and the mother and father of the human race. My writings aren't really that different. The way I understand it, angels (mostly female) were sent here to bear children fathered by humans. In essence, they were the mothers of the new race. No matter how one views the writings, there is no doubt, they are not boring.

In another of my writings, Ankar and Ye told of the Aborigines. Əfero's guardian was an aboriginal person from another land. He belonged to a tribe that was named the "Andreannar." They were the "Nameless Ones." No single person had a spoken name. His people did not speak. The ability to speak wasn't lacking, they just found it unnecessary. These people had the ability to communicate with mental telepathy, even at great distances.

They seemed to have complete control over their emotions and would be perceived as cold and without feeling. The contrary was true. They were highly emotional, but never let it be evident on the surface. They exhibited the classic poker face. It was a protective mechanism. If one was sensitive to them, as they were to each other, one could feel their emotions. Əfero had that ability. She was able to communicate mentally with her aboriginal guard. His people were courageous, and quite honorable. The appearance I visualize is like that of the aboriginal people of Australia. I have always found them a beautiful people.

I was curious where Əfero's guardian came from, so I asked Ankar. He wrote,

> *It was a faraway place. It was a place accessible by few others and kept secret from all. You see, he was a Nameless One, he was a secret people. He was from*

The New Race—Adam and Eve Revisited

the silent people. They were a very ancient people. Yes, they were of the aboriginal tribe. They were a very sacred people to God; his chosen people. This was their belief, and it was true, although God loved all his people. Then the Andreannar tribes were His chosen, because they were of the spirit. They were sacred. They were truly enlightened. They knew God.

I believe he came from Australia. We must keep in mind this was fifteen thousand years ago. With earthquakes and volcanic activity, the earth's surface could have been different then. Australia could have been closer to India, or even Africa. For all we know, Australia could have been the island continent between India and Africa. It could have been Lemuria, although I personally don't think this to be so. I believe Australia could have been closer to Africa and India, but I also believe there was a separate island or continent that could have been Lemuria.

Whatever the case may be, the writings tell us that the aboriginal people of Australia inhabited that part of the earth for at least fifteen thousand years. I believe they are survivors, and they have changed very little in their abilities and their appearance. They are a very special people. As providence would have it, a few years after writing the first draft of this book, I took a class at the university that was called Native American Myth and Oral Tradition. In that class was a visiting aboriginal person from Australia. So, I was able to learn more about the aboriginal Australians without having to go to Australia. However, I still hope to go to Australia to learn more about them.

The angels were obviously a special group of earth's inhabitants at that time. Ankar and Ye told me that to be of the temple, one must be anointed. To be anointed, one must have been of angelic descent. To be half angel and half human was an honor and placed one in a position of superiority. To be pure angel placed one in an enviable position, indeed. The angels were looked upon as special, advanced, almost, if not in fact, superhuman. This is why it was believed an advanced race of people would be born, and so they were.

This makes me wonder about many things. I think about white supremacy. I think about Hitler and his super race. Did the myths of the Greek gods come from this, or other mythologies involving gods and goddesses from cultures much older than that of Greece?

After doing some reading, I was quite surprised to find, written in the Bible, mention of the angels living on the earth. Could the attitude of bigotry stem from this? The thought of other planets and their inhabitants coming to earth with similar ideas crosses my mind, as well. Perhaps these other planetary races were warring with one another here on earth, and that is what caused the holocaust. The writings continued to say that this new race was just beginning to come to life when the holocaust came.

Chapter 8

The Holocaust

The end of Lemuria came suddenly. It seems it took very little time for all to be lost. It's controversial as to what caused the destruction. I've heard it was a natural disaster. It stands to reason that an earthquake could have caused the breakup of the land mass.

Geologists have determined a great growth plate phenomenon. These growth plates are found mostly on the ocean floor. Between the growth plates are fissures from which molten rock arises and cools. This causes the plates to spread apart and make room for the newly formed rock. This is called "Plate Tectonics." One of these lines extends from the Atlantic Ocean through the Mediterranean Sea, down through the Red Sea, and on through the Indian Ocean. Consequently, much seismic activity would have been taking place directly under Lemuria.

My writings tell of a group of powerful people who attacked Lemuria to take it as their own. I believe

Ankar and Ye have been trying to tell me the "anglomen" are responsible. I believe they are also trying to make it clear to me, this same group, the "anglomen," are preparing to do the same thing again. Evidently, that's the reason I'm here; to save the world from this disaster. At any rate, when the "anglomen" attacked Lemuria, they were the cause of its total destruction.

In a book my oldest brother purchased, was written a story very similar to what I had written. It went into detail as to the destruction of Lemuria, as well as other areas. The book stated nuclear fission was used for peaceful means for a long period of time during the life of Atlantis and Lemuria. The book had mentioned a group of people that had become greedy and land hungry. These people wanted to rule all the earth. They had realized the ability of nuclear fission as a weapon and deployed its use in missiles. These missiles caused the complete annihilation of Lemuria.

While I was writing I received images of the events that took place. Through the eyes of an eighteen-year-old Əfero, I saw the temple shaking, much like an earthquake. The ground was shaking and the temple was breaking up. Rocks were falling and the beams were beginning to collapse under the pressure.

The high priestess and the other maidens of the temple were in the altar room praying. Əfero's guard quickly clutched her arm and pulled her from her room. He ran with her to the outside at the temple entrance. A guard came running with Gentrana from the inside of the temple. The guard and Əfero's guardian ran back into the temple to try to save the others. Əfero and her sister latched onto one another as if to never let go. The panic occurring all around them was palpable.

Once outside the temple, they could see the people screaming and running around without direction. The earth began to vibrate under their feet, and everything began to shake again. In horror, they watched the temple entrance crumble. Dust from the collapsing entrance began to fill the air where they were standing. It was evident that no one else would be coming out.

Hand in hand they ran away from the buildings. They didn't know where they were going. They just ran in a direction that would take them away from the falling debris. Əfero turned to look behind her as they ran. The buildings were breaking apart and falling to the ground in pieces. The dust was thick. She could also see a huge ball of fire hit the ground and the earth shook. When the fire ball hit, it rolled out like a carpet in all directions, consuming everything in its path. There was nowhere to run to escape it. Gentrana and Əfero tried to run faster, but they were no match for the wall of fire approaching. It only took a few seconds for the fire to reach them and they were gone. That is where my vision abruptly ended.

From the description of the events that took place at that time, I have three possibilities of what could have occurred to cause the demise of Lemuria. One, it could have been an earthquake that caused volcanic activity, or vice versa. Two, it could have been an attack from a hostile group looking to take over. We have no proof as to whether or not there existed the knowledge and technology to develop and produce nuclear weapons. We don't know how advanced the people were at that time. Just as today, we live in a highly technological society, while in other parts of the world still exist people who wear loincloths and hunt with spears. Who's to say that at the time there lived the "cave man," there weren't also advanced civilizations living elsewhere on the planet? Three, a giant meteor could have hit the land. The impact and heat could have caused the devastation of Lemuria.

Edgar Cayce also spoke of warfare being the cause of the destruction of Atlantis and Lemuria. He spoke of laser weapons, as opposed to nuclear missiles. All the incidents spoke of or written about by Edgar Cayce, resulted in the same end, annihilation of the lands of the earth.

Whatever the cause, Lemuria was destroyed, without a trace, that we know of. All we have to go on are the legends and myths handed down. I believe legends and myths are created from some factual source. They had to start somewhere, for some reason.

The Holocaust

How much the present-day version deviates from the original, we have no way of knowing.

As stories are passed down through the ages, certain parts can be twisted and distorted to add interest or fit to the person who is telling the story. I do know that with the Native American story tellers, it is vitally important and required that the story be unchanged. The stories have to be "to the word" throughout time. Unfortunately, this may not have been the case with the myths and stories pertaining to Lemuria and Atlantis. Then again, perhaps it is. All we have to go on is with what we have. However, what we have isn't a great deal. I feel if my writings are telling me about Lemuria, there is reason to believe it did exist.

Cracking the Angels' Code

Chapter 9

The Pact—Your Mission, Should You Choose to Accept It...

We will presume that Lemuria was destroyed by the anglomen. This brings us to the point of why I am here, according to the angels. Ye and Ankar tell me that a pact was made by me and others. We made a pact to keep coming back until we stopped the anglomen. To date, I'm not sure who is involved or included. Ye and Ankar tell me there are those who are involved, and those who agreed to come at certain times and help on the physical level. It seems all who were of the temple have some part. Perhaps it's only those of angelic descent who are in the actual pact. Whoever they are, all are supposed to be on the earth at this time.

Evidently, we had many past lives together in an attempt to "save the world." Those anglomen must be pretty cunning, because we haven't succeeded yet. I guess we just kept getting wiped out on the way. We must live by the old adage, "If at first you don't succeed, try, try, again." (After fifteen thousand years, maybe we wrote that old adage.) Ye and Ankar kept stressing the fact the world needed saving and we are here to do it.

Warnings and protection were always being given from Ankar and Ye. They would be there for me whenever I needed them, as well as for others. On November 2, 1988, I had a very interesting writing experience.

> Who is with me now?
>
> *Ankar and Ye. ...Please be leery of those that say they are of the light and are not. They can lie to you, please be careful. ...You are here to save the world. You are here to save the world. Go and be at peace. You are doing just fine. Love always. Ankar and Ye*
>
> What do you mean save the world?
>
> *You are here to rid the world of evil, of all that is bad, and all that is not in the best interest of those who are here to better themselves. You are not going to go out and kill anyone.* (Well, I'm certainly glad of that!) *You are just going to expose them. You will make people see that they are not as they seem. They are*

The Pact—Your Mission, Should You Choose to Accept It...

> *not as they seem, and they take advantage of those who are not at all in a leadership position; the followers. You are the leaders who are needed, and you will always prevail.*

Is there anyone we should be leery of in particular?
> *Yes, but you must find out for yourself. You must find out for yourself.* (I believe this is part of my learning to discern people and situations.)

How long will it be?
> *It will be a little while longer, and all will make sense to you, all will make sense to you. May you go in peace, Ɵfero. You will soon see that all is real, all is true, all is as we have said, all is as we have said.*

Ankar had been writing a great deal to me. Ye seemed to have taken a back seat to him. All I knew about Ankar is that he suddenly showed up one day. He told me that the temple was the "Temple of Ankar," and that was all I had to go on. What exactly did that mean? I have this entity telling me to save the world, and I don't even know who he is. I decided I'd get a few things clarified.

Ankar, was it your temple that Ɵfero was in?
> *Yes, it was. It was my temple, and you were my special angel. You see, you were chosen to be my*

spokesperson. You were chosen to be the voice of Ankar.

How could I (Əfero) be the voice of Ankar? Əfero was never seen by anyone.

You were seen on holy days. You were heard from on those days.

What did Əfero do?

You were the voice of Ankar. You are the voice of Ankar today. (I'm the voice of Ankar today?)

Am I Ankar?

No. You are Əfero. You are the chosen one. (of-course... okay...)

Who or what are you, Ankar?

I am the god of the temple. I am the messenger to the people. (You're a messenger?)

Messenger for whom?

MESSENGER FOR ME. (Whoa!! Who is this? What a powerful presence in the pen.)

Who is "me"?

I AM THE HOLY OF HOLY. I AM. (I think we're talking God here. If there is a God, I think I just got a direct line. There's a great deal of power here. I can feel it in the pen. Yes, folks, not only do I write in tongues, I channel God.

Maybe it's just my big ego showing itself. Then again, maybe it is God. Right Irene, dream on. Maybe it's just another part of me.)

At the time this message was written to me, I had no idea there was an "I Am." However, shortly after this writing, out of the blue a book fell off my book shelf in front of me. It was one from a pile of books a friend gave me. I hadn't even looked at them, but I put the pile on the shelf to have them out of the way. When I picked up the book that fell to the floor, I looked at it. I stood there shocked when I read the cover: The "I AM" Discourses, by Godfrey Ray King. When I opened the book and read a bit about it, I was floored.

I asked the powerful entity, the "Holy of Holy," if he (it?) was a part of me.

Are you also a part of me?
(I could feel the difference in the pen again. Ankar started to write) *And, you thought you were alone.* (Funny Ankar, real funny.)

What did this mean? Are we "The Chosen," on a mission from God? Is this possible? Why do I suddenly feel like Joan of Arc? If I believed, and had the faith Joan of Arc possessed, I think I'd know just how she felt, and what she went through.

The way I felt at the time I wrote this, I feel somewhat like that today, I had to ask myself a very important question. Why me? If this is a mission from

God, how did I end up a part of it? I have no religious convictions. At the time I received these writings, I wrote the following excerpt in the first draft of the manuscript of this book: "I'm sure I'm not considered a holy person. Okay, maybe the psychic at my first fair thought I was holy. I don't see anyone breaking down my door to be blessed or healed or anything."

As I look back and review the transition of my reclusive life to the life I have today, (I still have a reclusive nature, but I am out in the world), I see a dramatic difference. I am more educated now. This education initially came from book learning and life experience, and culminated in the education for my Ph.D.

In retrospect, I recall incidences that lead me to realize, I am in fact a "Holy Person." I mean this as a sense of presence perceived but not understood by others, and many times resulted in a person fearing me on some level. I'm not exactly sure where it comes from, but it is definitely a presence, especially to people who are sensitive. I've noticed, on some strange level, this presence I carry is most evident to men (and probably people in general) who have something to hide, or live surrounding themselves with a negative energy of one kind or another.

There are a couple of instances that stand out to me. A few years after I wrote the original draft of this book, I was in Belgium visiting a friend. While there, I found myself suddenly thrust into a double date situation. The two men were from Morocco. The man who was my "date," was very nervous with me. While we were making small talk (we knew nothing about each other), I noticed him doing his best to stay on the very edge of the booth seat we shared, so he would not be too close to me. I guess I looked at him perplexed, and he said to me, "I cannot touch you. You are a holy woman." He then proceeded to state how he would protect me that night. His reaction to me, and what he said, threw me.

Another incident happened in this country, in Los Angeles. I was talking to a public relations person about promoting me to get my name out there for my psychic and astrology work. I wanted to be recognized when I submitted the second iteration of my book. He was quite used to dealing with the "wanna-be starlets" that would do "anything" to get a part in a film or television.

After we talked about the possible outlets for promotion, he walked me to my car. At the car, he told me he didn't know whether to hug me or not touch me at all and protect me as I left the parking area. He told me he didn't know what to think of me and the situation, because he'd never been with someone like me. His reaction and behavior made me think again about the incident in Belgium.

I do find it interesting that I seem to scare the hell out of men. I guess that's why I'm still single. Maybe there is something to what the man in Belgium said to me. Certainly, everyone I meet doesn't treat me that way, but it happens often enough.

I think, even to this day, I don't feel worthy of such a position as Ankar and Ye have told me I have. Then again, that's probably past programming. The Catholics are big on guilt. I didn't understand then, and I still have a bit of a problem accepting that I am supposed to be one of the chosen. It was apparent through my writings; I was the only one having a problem with this.

Basically, everyone was telling me to get it together. I had a job to do, so do it. I was reminded a few times I was wasting precious time. On occasion, Ye and Ankar would lose patience with me over this. One incident was November 16, 1988.

> Who is with me?
>> *Ye and Ankar. You have taken a long time to write to us. What is wrong Əfero? You see, we are here to guide you. You are not allowing us to do that for you, or with you. Can't you see that? Can't you see that your time is short? Your time is short.*
>
> What do you mean, my time is short?
>> *Your time is short. You are wasting precious time. You should be out among the people. You should be exposing the wrong doers. You must go do the things you came here to do. You must go.*
>
> What can I do?

The Pact—Your Mission, Should You Choose to Accept It...

You can expose those who would cause evil and havoc among the people. You can write and put things on television. You can do many things. You are here for this purpose. Can you see the importance? Anything that you can do will help you. You can come home to the great place and forget about all of this, but you made a pact to do this. You have all that you need. You have all that you need. You can use the media to show the people that not all is as it seems. You can expose those who have already taken advantage of the people. You can show them for what they are. You have everything you need. You are backed by the supreme energy. Educate the people. Educate the people. You can find many answers on the mountain at the site of the angel. It is here that the secrets are revealed. It is here where the answers are kept. Go, go to the mountain, much awaits you there.

Where is the mountain?

The mountain is at your caverns, Ǝfero. You have been there in this life. You have been there. It is Mount Shasta, and the ancient one is there. You will find him. He has been waiting for you. He has waited for eons. Now you can go to do the things you came here to do. You and others have made the pact to come back and change the world.

At the time this writing took place, I had not yet been given the book *I AM*. I knew nothing about Mt.

Shasta other than it was "my mountain" as I referred to it as a kid. I fell in love with the caverns not far from the mountain.

> Where will I find the ancient one?
> *He will find you. He will find you.*

You just wrote that I would find him. Please elaborate.

> *Əfero, you are always full of questions and disbelief. Sometimes I wonder how you were to become the chosen one.* (That makes two of us) *Have you lost all of your faith? Have you lost sight of all you have worked for, and all you have learned? Əfero, go to the mountain, and the ancient one will be there. Things will be much more clear to you then. You are very special, Əfero. You are truly of the light. The light of supreme energy; of God. We are so blessed to have Əfero with us.* (OH! BROTHER!! but thanks. I'm really the lucky one you guys, and don't you forget it!)

Thanks for all the flattery guys, but I have a couple more questions. When is the best time to go to Mount Shasta?

> *Go when the weather permits. Go when you can get through. Plan this trip. You can use it to your best advantage. You can use it for part of your story. Go, and good luck, Ankar and Ye.*

The Pact—Your Mission, Should You Choose to Accept It...

One time, Ye and Ankar did not want to write to me. I think they were a little upset with me.

Do you guys want to talk to me?
No, we don't. (What? They never said no.)

Why?
Because you are always asking questions, and never acting on the answers and information that we give you. You can do so much, but you don't. You don't. You can make a difference in the world, but you are lazy. You waste time. You waste precious time. Can't you see that? You can try and contact the people who publish books. You can contact the people who produce television programs. You have a wonderful and wide selection of choices available to you. You must do what you came to do. You must do what you came to do. (I think that is as close as one can get to being chewed-out by an entity.)

I think they are real serious about this mission thing, or is it just me? I thought this was really letting me have it. Obviously to them, I was not getting the message. They did not give up on me. No, they were not going to let me get off easy. They pulled in the big guns. Ankar and Ye thought they could shake me up, and so they did, in December 1988.

Who is with me now?

This is Ye and Adama and Ankar and Me. (Adama, as in the father of Ɵfero?)

Who is me?
Let me tell you something... (scribbling starts and I cut it off)

Are you of the light? (I thought I had better get this out of the way.)
Yes. Are you of the light? Are you? (What is this?)

I think so. If the light is good, then I am of the light. Are you?
Yes, Ɵfero. Can you understand that to do this we must know that we can trust each other? We must be able to trust each other.

Who are you?
I am. I am the head of the council of the angelic order. Can you understand this? (Kind of) *This is Archangel Michael.* (Hey, why not? Everybody else seems to be dropping in.)

I'm sorry, but I find that difficult to believe, but what do you want to communicate to me?
We need to start a new group of level two people. These people can aid us on a lower aspect of this mission. Can we start with a group of lesser angels? We will let you know now that the mission will not be an easy one. For you are to read the letters that

The Pact—Your Mission, Should You Choose to Accept It...

were written to the Pope, by those who would rape the earth, and the related ancestors to the original of the angelic order.

Who are they?
This is up to you to find out. This will be your first mission. Can you do this?

Can I do what?
Can you find the answers about him? He has been around the area of super ageless. (I cut him off. This was just getting to be too much. Do I look like Dick Tracy? Come on, get real. I can't do this stuff.)

If I found this all difficult to believe before, this topped it. How in the world am I supposed to go to Rome, and find letters to the Pope? Besides, I'm not sure if it was Archangel Michael writing me.

Then I began to think, maybe it's not me personally who is supposed to go to Rome. Maybe they mean that I am supposed to give the information to someone. If this was the case, to whom was I supposed to give the information?

There must be those of the chosen who are in a position to take action. I gather the information and give it to them. Now, this does make more sense. Yes, it's what Ankar wrote. He was the messenger to the people. I was his voice then, as I am his voice now. I am the messenger. Maybe that's what this is about.

Chapter 10

Revelation, The Angels Are Among Us

I had done a great deal of thinking about what Ankar and Ye were communicating to me. They certainly had me on the go trying to comprehend their messages. I am one who delves deeply into subjects, and I can analyze them to death. From my writings, I came up with several theories. I felt there was a connection with something in the *Bible*, something in "Revelation." I was unfamiliar with the content in the New Testament, but I just knew, intuitively, there was a connection to what Ankar and Ye were telling me and the "Book of Revelation."

Quite honestly, I was afraid to read it because it might influence my writing. As it was, I could claim no prior knowledge of anything coming to me through the communication with Ye and Ankar. If I did have

Cracking the Angels' Code

prior knowledge of a subject, I really questioned it, because I could have written it subconsciously.

A great deal of time past before I finally read the "Book of Revelation." I might not have read it for a longer period of time, had it not been for a movie I'd seen on television. I saw previews to a movie called *The Seventh Sign*. I thought it was going to be about some metaphysical phenomena. It sparked my interest, and I decided I would watch it. I was in for quite a surprise.

The movie, *The Seventh Sign*, was the slap in the face I needed. It was the answer to the question, "What could one woman do to save the world?" Too, it was symbolic. At the time, I questioned if it was fate that I saw the preview to that movie and determined to watch it. Now, I see it more as synchronicity. The film definitely had an impact on me.

It was after that movie that I went to the *Bible* and read the "Book of Revelation." I had many of my own "revelations" after reading it. At the time I wrote the original manuscript for this book, I read the "Book of Revelation" from a literal perspective, and that is how I made the connections and interpretations I share in this chapter.

The tie-in with my writings was incredible. I was overwhelmed with the correlation between the two. Could it be? Could it be that what I am writing is following the "Book of Revelation"? Could this truly be the "end time"? Is that why my time is short? Is that

Revelation, The Angels Are Among Us

why they say I'm here to save the world? Am I a messenger angel? Or am I one of the seven angels with the vials as mentioned in "Revelation"? All kinds of thoughts were racing through my mind.

I had done some figuring through the writings that there must have been twelve of the chosen; twelve angels in the pact. There were also twelve main angels in "Revelation." There were the seven trumpet angels, the angel with the censor, and the four cherubim. I knew I was really reaching in the dark on this one. What a comparison I had going on, me and the angels of "Revelation." It was all so overwhelming. Why was this all happening now? Was there a relation between my writings and "Revelation"? I decided to ask Ankar and Ye about all of this on Christmas morning 1988.

Who is there?
Adama.

Can I ask a question about the group of twelve?
Yes, you can. You are correct. There are twelve.

Are all twelve identified?
No, only eight. There are also more helpers, several more.

Do I still need to go to the mountain? (I had been putting this off out of fear.)
Yes, it is important that you see the ancient one. It is also important that you see a man at the science

> room. This is a person who can help you. He has been studying about what is to take place. All is not as it seems. All is not as it seems.

What do you mean all is not as it seems? With who, what?
> You have much to learn yet. You have much to learn. You have much to see, read, and hear. You have got to go see the ancient one. He can tell you much that can open your mind to what is going on in the world.

Can you tell me what is the deadline? Can you tell me what will happen if I don't do anything? (Because that is seriously what I was thinking I would do . . . nothing!)
> A long time ago you knew what was happening to the world. You knew that there would be a day when all could be lost again. All could be lost or destroyed.

Is this to do with the "Book of Revelation" in the Bible?
> Yes and no. You see, you are facing a time when man is creating his own end. All is like a repeating of the past. When Jesus Christ came into this world, He too had a mission, He too was a chosen one, He too had a group of twelve. Can you see that this is the second coming? You are a part of something great. You are a part of something wonderful, but we must win to be

successful. Can you understand this? Can you see who you are?

As I read this excerpt now, from the perspective of the educated Irene, knowing that there is little solid evidence pertaining to the existence of "Jesus," I put on my skeptical/scrutinizing hat while still doing my best to keep an open mind. However, I also understand the concept of ascended and spiritual masters, among which "Jesus" may be included.

The more I read the "Book of Revelation," the more awestruck I became. I began relating events that I had written about, to those that have already taken place, and are taking place today. The devastating oil spills caused the death of many living souls (creatures) in the sea.

Of the oil spills that happen around the world, the Alaskan oil spill of 1989 did not have the usual oil spill look. The oil congealed and formed like clots in the ocean, much as the blood of a "dead man." The pollution of our lakes, bays, and waterways has caused them to look like blood. The depletion of the ozone layer allowed the dangerous rays of the sun to get through and reach the earth's surface. It caused more damage to the skin, burning it, and creating tumors and sores. The slaughter of the whales has drastically reduced their number. The tuna industry has done its fair share in reducing the dolphin population. The comparison to "Revelation" is, of-course, my personal view. Perhaps it's just coincidence (Yeah, right). It certainly makes one think.

Some of my writings contained words and phrases identical to those in the *Bible*. Ankar and Ye mentioned the "ancient of days." They wrote of the "second coming." Then there was "the beginning of the end," after which there would be a "new heaven and a new earth." In January 1989, Ankar and Ye wrote a letter to my brother, in which they mentioned the gathering of the elders.

Who is with me?
Ankar and Ye.

What can you tell me, or is there another message for my brother?
Yes. He must take a chance to be at the capitol of the church of the people of God. He will know all at that time. He has a chance, to stop the kings of the world from acting on impulse and creating a new land for all nations in one. He can do this by going to the church that has the name of the best apostle of Christ. He will know.

Can you elaborate or be more specific? (They had a tendency to write in, what seemed like, metaphors or riddles. I was starting to feel like Nostradamus.)
He can be at the top of the list of the few that are chosen to represent Him. He is the one who can make

the change. For a thousand years a secret has been kept by those in power. They are a great strength, and they are a great greed.

Who are they?
They are the kings of men. They are the ones who take control and lead all who will follow.

At the time I wrote this, I had no idea or knowledge about the royal bloodlines and their alleged connections to what conspiracy theorists might call, the Illuminati. Perhaps Ye and Ankar were referring to this group. From what they wrote, it seems so.

Can you name names?
Yes, but that can cause much more trouble than being found out another way. All is not as it seems in the world. All is not as it seems.

Is there anything else you would like to tell my brother?
At this time, he must take steps to come along, and be in the place where the elders meet. He can then tell them of you, Əfero. He can tell them that you are the "Angel of Light," you are the chosen one, you are the savior. (This is really getting out there, as far as I'm concerned. It's got me on the edge of my seat but come on. The savior? I suppose, if I think about it, a savior is someone who saves others or things. If I'm here to be part of a team to save the

world, then I guess it does fit. I think I'll try and get some clarification.)

What do you mean?
All is well, Əfero. They must know how you have come to this being. He has sent you, and He has given another gift to the world. You can make the changes, Əfero. You can make the changes.

What am I to do?
You will know when the time is right. You have many around you at this time. They have come to aid you in this. You will be the leader of men. You will be the "dove" and "the way." Many are here to share the task. Many are here to support you. All is not as it seems. Go now and tell your brother what I have said here. He will start the beginning of the end. All will change soon, very soon, and a new earth will be the final result. Fear not, Əfero, all are here for you. All are here for you. All are ancient of days. You are the ancient one for the world. Go now. . . . tell him all, "all" that is written here. Ankar and Ye (They knew I was embarrassed to tell my brother about this stuff. They elaborated the "all," so I would be sure to leave nothing out.)

My brother knows many people. I suppose Ankar and Ye thought he could do something. Perhaps they thought he could "spread the word." They wrote to him several times to help him with certain things in his life. He told me they were correct about most everything they wrote to him. I was rather surprised about that, as I wrote earlier, they write in riddles sometimes. Evidently my brother understood. He thought he was here to help me. He thought, perhaps, he was one of the action people. I was told he was one of the helper angels; if not one of the original twelve. I don't know for sure. There was more to the "Revelation" connection than just the angels involved. Oftentimes one hears mentioned in Bible conversation "the mark of the beast." Which is usually then followed by "six, six, six."

After I read "Revelation," I realized that doesn't tell the whole story. If one reads "Revelation" 13:17-18, one will see there is a "mark," and there is a "number." The mark of the beast is not the same as the number. The number refers to a name. The line 13:17 includes, "the mark of the beast, his name, or the number of his name." Line 13:18 states, "Here is wisdom, let him that hath understanding count the number of the beast, for it is the number of a man, and his number is six hundred, threescore and six."

This started another thought to run through my mind. I have the understanding of numbers. Could it be that I am to expose the beast? Will I be the one with the wisdom and the ability? I doubt it. Certainly, any numerologist could do it. Why me?

If one thinks about it, what difference would it make? What would happen if someone did discover it? We would have the name of the beast, then what? Would that change the course of events? Would that save the world? If that's so, then how? Certainly, it would be interesting to try to determine just what the name is.

Looking at this from the perspective of the numerologist, tells me a great deal. As an astrologer, I could also see more in this than most. Interpreting these biblical lines, with the knowledge of numerology and astrology, brings interesting results when viewed from the English language.

Again, I was being very literal with what I was reading in the Bible. I know now that Biblical scholars see the symbolism in the words and phrases, but I lacked the education to interpret on that level. I still lack the education to interpret, yet I found myself on the trail of some interesting discoveries and was feeling a bit like Indiana Jones.

Numerologically speaking, we know the number 666 corresponds with the name of a man. One would have to have the knowledge of numerology for me to go into any detail. I can specify that "the beast" could have a first, middle, and last name, each one with a value of six. This would give us, the first name = 6, middle name = 6, last name = 6, thus the 666. Each letter of the alphabet, according to numerology, has its own numerical value. The number of the beast could also be the total of all the letters in the full name. Another point that should be made clear is there is more than one method of doing numerology. The method one uses may produce a different result.

I wanted to look at this astrologically as well. Taking it from the beast aspect, led me to look for an astrological sign represented by a beast. This gives me, Taurus, the bull, and Leo, the lion. I reverted back to numerology to take this a step further. F, O and X are the only letters with a value of six. A fox isn't really considered a beast, and there is no sign represented by a fox. I dropped the F, and this gave me ox. An ox could be a bull, or a beast. I still needed another 6-value letter to fit the "three 6 (666)" theory.

I began to wonder if there was another way to spell ox. Perhaps the Latin or Greek origin used an extra X or O. The dictionary was the resource I needed for this, so I looked it up. I had no idea what I would discover, or where this would lead me.

The first place I looked was under the word "OX." One of the definitions was taken from Bos "taurus," a castrated bull of domestic origin, used as a "beast" of burden; a draft animal. This brought up Taurus and beast. There was no Latin or Greek origin to ox.

I decided to look under "bull." Was I in for a surprise. There were three definitions for the word "bull." The first was what one would have expected, pertaining to bovine. The second was an eye opener. The Latin origin was "bulla," which meant a seal, anything round. The definition was, "An official document or decree, especially one from the Pope." As I read down the list of words on the dictionary page with "bull," I stumbled across "Bulla." I read the definition, "A round lead seal attached to an official document from the Pope." Another definition for "bull" was trickery, lie. I was amazed at what I was reading. Could it be the mark of the beast is the Bulla, or bull; the papal seal?

I realize I'm taking a big step to even suggest there is a remote possibility the Pope is the beast. I'm not suggesting this Pope is the beast. I merely mean, if this is indeed true, a Pope could be the beast. We will need to take it one step further. We need to establish the number of the name of the particular Pope. The name would have to result in 666. This would then suggest, the name attributed to the number would be a good candidate.

As I delved deeper, I realized this could tie into "Revelation" 13:16. This reads, "and he causeth all, both small and great, rich and poor, free and bond, to receive a mark in their right hand, or in their foreheads;" the mark being the "mark of the beast" or papal seal.

The mark can also be his name, or the number of his name. This could be accomplished by wearing a ring on the right hand, or by wearing a hat on the head. This is very similar to other secret societies and organizations. The Masons, for example, are known for the ring they wear, and as the Shriners, the hat and symbol they wear. To wear a name, could simply mean going by a certain title. Again, the Masons call themselves Masons. Perhaps, to wear the name of the beast would be a simple matter of being a Catholic or being recognized as such. The mark could be baptismal water placed on the forehead.

Another point must be made here. There is more than one beast in "Revelation." "Revelation" 13:11-16 states:

13:11 "And I beheld another beast coming up out of the earth.; and he had two horns like a lamb and he spake like a dragon."

13:12 "And he exerciseth all the power of the first beast before him, and causeth the earth and them that dwell therein to worship the first beast whose deadly wound was healed."

13:13 "And he doeth great wonders, so that he maketh fire come down from heaven on the earth in the sight of men." (Sounds a little like the destruction of Lemuria in my vision.)

13:14 "And deceiveth them that dwell on the earth by those miracles which he had power to do in the sight of the beast, which had the wound by a sword and did live."

13:15 "And he had power to give life unto the image of the beast, that the image of the beast should both speak, and cause that as many as would not worship the image of the beast would be killed." (This is reminiscent of the Spanish Inquisition.)

The first beast was like a puppet to the second beast. It is the number and the number of the name of the first beast that is mentioned, not the second. If a Pope were the beast, he would be the first beast. The real "bad guy" is the second beast. Whoever he is or will be. While I'm at it, I want to make it clear, these were only my personal observations and theories at that time. I still find them very interesting, though.

Chapter 11

The Mountain

Throughout my writings I have been told to go to the mountain. I live in Northern California, about a three-hour drive from Mount Shasta. I was there once, or at least near there, when I was in the eighth grade. My eighth-grade class toured the Shasta caverns. It was a wonderful experience, as I had never seen caverns before. As wonderful as it was, I didn't have a religious experience, or see God, or anything even close. I just simply loved the beauty of it all.

I had heard a few times, after my eighth-grade excursion, UFOs had been sighted there. There were other stories about extraterrestrials living on the mountain. I've never gone to investigate, and I didn't know anyone who had. I never really had a desire to go for that purpose. I would have liked to have gone to tour the caverns again, but that had been the extent of my desire.

Ye told me to go to the mountain in August of 1988. After that particular writing, I had forgotten all about it. When I was told again to go to the mountain, they didn't say which mountain. I still didn't remember the first writing, and never re-read any of what I had written. So, it was a mystery to me what mountain they wanted me to go to.

My brother, who knew I was getting these messages, thought Ye and Ankar wanted me to go to a mountain in the Philippines. He had spent a great deal of time in the Philippines during his time in the military. He told me of the mountain he had gone to while he was there. He told me of the caves with very small openings. It is said the openings are too small for people to fit through. He told me the openings grow large enough to fit those who are special. If one is a member of the select, or chosen, if you will, the openings seem to mysteriously become large enough to accommodate one's stature.

Once inside the cave, one sees an altar with various religious articles. Catholicism is the major Christian religion in the Philippines. Evidently, strange spiritual encounters are supposed to take place while in the caves. There are those who have claimed to have become enlightened and blessed while there, and others who are endowed with special abilities, such as healing and clairvoyance.

My brother was one of the select chosen. He was able to fit through an opening and gain access to a cave. He never revealed to me what spiritual phenomena he encountered while in the cave. He merely told me of the altar.

He did tell me there was an old man on the mountain. The old man lived up there. The man presented himself to my brother and led him to his home. His living conditions appeared to be very primitive. During his visit with the man, my brother was given an amulet. It was a triangular shaped piece with symbols on it. It is for my brother's protection, and he feels very strongly about it.

It was because of all of this that my brother thought the mountain in the Philippines was the mountain I was supposed to go to. He thought the old man who gave him the amulet was the "ancient one" Ye and Ankar were telling me I needed to see. It certainly did make sense, and it seemed to fit with the description. However, Ye and Ankar wrote again that the mountain was Mount Shasta.

They had described the mountain as the one with the angels and the caves. Helen had told me that the previous year, she and her family had gone to Oregon. While driving from Oregon into California, she could see Mount Shasta. She said there was a cloud formation above the mountain. She saw an angel in the clouds and brought it to the attention of her family. Each of the family members had also seen it. To her it was very special. To have Ankar and Ye mention it brought back her memory of the incident. She told me she knew immediately what they meant. She was sure the mountain was Mount Shasta.

I couldn't help but wonder just what to expect there. Throughout time, mountains have been places of mystery. Different cultures share the same reverence for mountains. Often mountains have been places where one goes to communicate with one's god. The lamas of Tibet live on the mountain, high in the Himalayas. In Greek mythology, the gods actually resided on a mountain—Mount Olympus. There are stories about the "Great White Brotherhood," "The Seven Rays," and "The Ascended Masters," all of who make their homes in various mountains around the world (as I understand it). In the *Bible*, Moses received the commandments and talked with God on a mountain. In fact, there are many incidents in the *Bible* that involve mountains. What could possibly await me on Mount Shasta?

I have read books involving people's experiences while on Mount Shasta. In one particular book, the people involved received messages to go there. The messages they received were very similar to mine. I found this to be true in different books I have read, as well as listening to the accounts of other peoples' experiences. This affirmed to me, I was not alone in being given a message to "go to the mountain." I was not unique. It was a comfort to know there were others. At the same time, it was also frightening to me to have another aspect of my writings confirmed.

Again, I asked myself, "Could this all be true? Could all that I have written really be true? Is the world going to go through some great change? Is there going to be another holocaust like Lemuria?" The thought is unpleasant and concerning, but depending on one's perspective, it could be a positive thing. Maybe the change will mean there will be a change in thought consciousness. Perhaps it means that the vibration rate of the souls on earth will rise. Maybe the planet itself will change.

During the time I first started writing this book (August 1989), I delayed and put off visiting the mountain. The main reason for that was because I was afraid of what I might find there. If I did meet with the "ancient one," perhaps I would have learned of things that would have caused me grief. I may have found all that I had written was true. The information I received may have involved the deaths of the people I know and love.

Within the writings there was mention of nuclear or chemical accidents, and even global warfare; many deaths were likely. The thought of other possibilities crossed my mind as well. It was possible that I would learn how to avoid these things. Maybe I could learn of ways to make a change; save the world, if you will.

At that time, I had a great fear of death. I've grown and learned so much since then. We, in our physical bodies die, but our energy self lives on. We merely move from one type of life to another. I don't claim to have all the answers, I simply have come to a sense of peace within. I've connected, even if only slightly, to that space of knowingness that resides in each of us.

In November 1995, I finally did go to the mountain. I really didn't know what to expect, especially after so much time had passed since I was first told to go. I felt a little bad about that, but again, I had to keep in my mind that everything happens for a reason. I thought it appropriate to go on Thanksgiving. Even though it was eight years after the fact, I just decided I had to go. Even if there was no one there anymore, I wanted to go experience the majestic beauty of the area. I stayed for three days, and it was beautiful.

While in the area, I spent an afternoon on the mountain itself. I didn't run into any ancient looking old people, nor did a Lemurian stop me on my way. However, I merely allowed myself to experience the moment. I focused on the "here and now" with only myself and the trees with the earth beneath my feet. I connected my spirit with that of the mountain. I felt a part of it, a part of it all.

I realized my connection to all of nature and the planet I lived on. We are all made up of the same "raw materials." It is in the fruits from the trees that, with their roots, absorb nutrients from the ground. We eat the fruit, and it becomes a part of us. We are our planet. We are all things, and all things are us. Each thing we do that affects or hurts the earth in some way, affects and hurts us. If we kill our planet we kill ourselves.

My vibration rate must have been very high. My time on the mountain seemed like an everyday experience, perhaps just a little special. However, it wasn't until I left the area that I realized there had been some effect on my physical being. Perhaps it was initiated by the sensation of profound connectedness I felt to something elusive on the mountain. Even though I had plenty of sleep and exercise, within about four hours of driving back to southern California (where I was living at the time), I couldn't keep my eyes open. No reasonable explanation existed for the utter and complete exhaustion I was experiencing, and it was only eight o'clock at night! I had to stop and sleep.

I found a hotel on the way, paid for a room, and immediately fell asleep. I slept soundly through the night. I woke still feeling the connectedness I had felt on the mountain the day before. Unfortunately, shortly after returning to normal everyday life, I lost that "spiritual high." What a gift I was given while I was there. I will return to Mount Shasta one of these days, and who knows, maybe the "ancient one" will be there. Then again, maybe the "ancient one" was there, and he or she was with me the whole time.

While at a gathering of UFO experiencers, I shared the story of the "ancient one" and my Mount Shasta trip. One of the people at the gathering was sharing what he was visualizing as I told them my story. I have to share it with you, because I found it so funny.

He said he saw this very old man with worn and ragged clothes, and very long weather blown white hair, waiting for me on Mount Shasta. The old man was watching me as I approached. He was holding his arm out in the sunlight to get the necessary position. Flustered, he repeatedly pointed at the small "sundial" strapped to his wrist. Impatient and obviously anxious he said, "Do you know how long I've been waiting here for you? Do you have any idea what time it is? When they said you have a tendency to be late, they weren't kidding!"

Chapter 12

What?! I've Been Here Before?—Plotting Astrology on Maps

In late September 1989, I was in for a huge discovery. It had to do with a special kind of astrology involving maps. This was a discovery that would lead not only to the expansion of my astrological offerings, but also a personal discovery that would leave me a bit dumbfounded. This experience occurred while I was working a show, a large wholistic fair, held in a convention center in Sacramento, CA.

I was still a newbie in the professional world, and I shared a table at the fair with my friend and colleague, Helen. She had been a professional for a few years and was reading tarot. I was reading runes and adding a little astrology. During a lull in the crowd, I decided to take a quick run around the corner to a booth facing the walkway behind our row of tables. The booth was being run by an astrologer friend, Sam, who was selling astrology software. I stopped by to say hello and chat for a few minutes while the crowd was thin.

There was another person there manning the booth with Sam. I didn't recognize him, so Sam introduced him to me. His name was Wayne, and he was doing demonstrations with the software showing a special feature that involved maps. He called it, "Astro*Carto*Graphy," a form of astrology developed in the 1970s by a man named Jim Lewis. Wayne knew Jim Lewis and learned this mapping technique from him. Being a girl who was in love with maps, the world, travel, and everything to do with astrology, I was immediately intrigued.

Wayne asked me for my birth information. He entered it into the software. As he was looking at the screen, he became excited and a huge smile broke across his face. He printed a map. He grabbed the printout and said, "Look at this!" To my surprise, the map he printed was of the Middle East. He was referring to the area as Persia! What?! Was I hearing this man correctly?

Wayne was telling me that I may have had one or more past lives in what was Persia. I looked at the printout in utter amazement. I stood there spellbound as he told me the meaning of the planetary lines running up and down the map along longitude lines. I understood him to convey that the broken vertical lines can represent one's past life and solid vertical lines can represent one's present life.

According to the three lines on this map, my Venus (♀) line (love, beauty, values), my Sun (☉) line (personality, leadership, loyalty), and my Mercury (☿) line (communication, messenger, mental energy) went through parts of what had been Persia. In my personal astrology chart, all these planets are in the sign, Gemini (quick witted, orator, thinker). Gemini rules the lungs, shoulders, arms, and hands. I am relaying the astrological associations here so you will be able to have a bit of a grasp of what Wayne was about to tell me.

On the map, Wayne put his finger on the top left where Turkey was situated. He said, "This is your Venus line on the IC [past life line] going through Turkey, down through Cyprus, and continuing down right through Mount Sinai." He went on to say, "St. Catherine's Cathedral is on Mount Sinai." He told me that St. Catherine was a Catholic martyr, and they cut off her hands (Gemini). Supposedly, the relic of her hands is still there at the monastery.

I was a bit taken aback. I looked at Wayne and asked, "Are you saying that I might have been St. Catherine in a past life?" He didn't respond with a yes or a no. He was just excited about how coincidental and interesting it was. Even now as I revisit this, I have

Cracking the Angels' Code

to agree, it was very interesting. Needless to say, I immediately fell in love with Astro*Carto*Graphy.

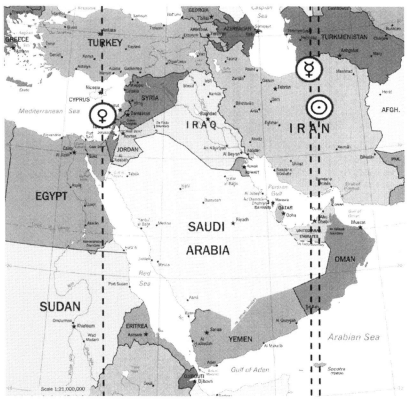

Map 2. Middle East with planetary lines.

Wayne went on to say that there were ancient ruins (temples to Aphrodite) in Western Turkey and my Venus line was close enough to have significance. And, isn't it uncanny that the line of my Venus (Aphrodite) was near a ruin that was once a temple to Aphrodite. Wayne explained three aspects of the meaning of Venus, they include "materializing values,

What?! I've Been Here Before?—Plotting Astrology on Maps

something precious, important relationship." I was transfixed on the map and on Wayne.

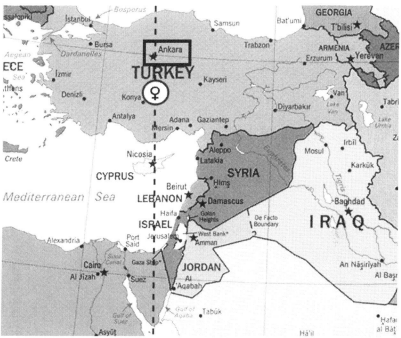

Map 3. Ankara, Turkey.

What I didn't realize until later, after looking at a more expansive map, that there were two important areas on the map that I didn't see when I was standing there with Wayne. First, I didn't see how close my Venus line was to Ankara. You may be wondering why that's important. According to Wayne, one of the meanings of Venus is an important relationship. If Ankara has any connection to the entity Ankar, then having my Venus line there could be an indication of the important relationship between myself and Ankar, which was materializing through the writing (which, now that I think of it, is an expression of Gemini). Naturally, this may be simply a fun coincidence, but the uncanny connections still have me pondering the phenomenon.

The second thing I missed when talking to Wayne that day was the location of Lemuria in relationship to my Sun (☉) and Mercury (☿) lines on the IC (past life lines). The lines go through the very western edge of where I see Lemuria to have been.

The line I haven't written about yet, is a line with the symbol (we call them glyphs in astrology) that looks like headphones (☊). This glyph represents the north node, what I refer to as your reason for coming into this world, or "your mission, should you choose to accept it." At the time, when Wayne was selling the astrology software, I don't believe the software had the option to plot the north node. It wasn't until later, with updates and improvements to the software, were the nodes a plotting option. Naturally, I bought that software and was able to determine the location of my nodes.

Simply because I understand astrology and figured out how the line positioning and layout would look, I knew that my north node would fall somewhere in Lemuria. In the case of this positioning, the north node is on an unbroken line, representing current lifetime. The line goes right through the western part of my vision of Lemuria. I couldn't help but wonder if my communication with the angels had something to do with my "mission" to bring some aspect of the story of Lemuria to life—to be a messenger, so to speak.

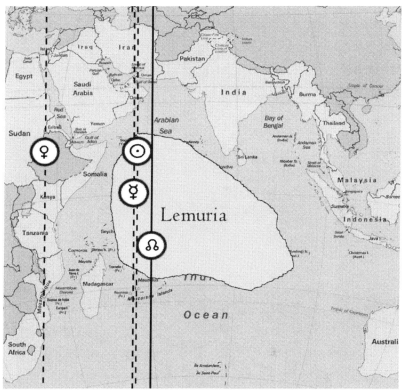

Map 4. Lemuria with planetary and node lines.

Just as I was awestruck when Wayne was first explaining my planetary lines, I was awestruck with what I was discovering here. Yet, this is only part of the story. All the planetary lines have a polar opposite. So, I expanded the map to find the location of those opposite lines. To my utter amazement, my node line on the IC (past life) ran directly through Mount Shasta! Yet again, I was utterly astounded.

The past life aspect of this node line still has me wondering what it means concerning Ǝfero. As far as I knew, she perished in her physical form when the fireball swept over her sister and her in Lemuria. At the time of this writing, in 2018, I still don't have any idea what the past life connection to Mount Shasta could have been.

Chapter 13

Validation—Is It True What They Say?

I have read several books that have validated a great deal of what I have written. Or, at the very least, they have similar information. Granted, some of the books are channeled, but that fact indicated that someone out there has tapped into something comparable to what I had tapped into. I am taken by the fact the information they received was the same or similar. The two most important books I've come across (so far) are the main focus of this chapter.

My first "slap in the face of reality" came just before Christmas in 1988. My oldest brother came up from Los Angeles about a week before Christmas. He brought a present for me. He wanted me to open the gift right away. He had found a book in a used bookstore. He thought I would find it interesting, so he bought it for my Christmas present.

The book was channeled. It was put out by the Urantia Foundation in 1955. The book was titled, *The Urantia Book*. It is a mammoth book, and it covers a vast amount of information on the universe, the angelic order, Adam and Eve, Jesus Christ, and more. It is supposedly written by angels and other celestials. It is fascinating to say the least.

My brother knew I had been writing, but at that time he knew very little about it. He had no idea of the contents, and no idea the impact his gift would have. We were both in for quite a surprise.

Before I had a chance to even look through my new book, my brother wanted to drive into town for something. On the way we started talking about angels. I told him about my writings from a few weeks earlier, that I was supposedly an angel in Lemuria. For some reason he asked if I had wings. I informed him the wings were removed because they weren't needed on earth. He looked at me with an awkward face and said, "Yeah, that's right." I realized he was shocked I knew about the wings being removed. I couldn't believe my brother knew what I was talking about.

When we returned home, my brother grabbed the book, and started showing me the parts on Lucifer and the fallen angels. I was more interested in the parts about Adam and Eve. I realized I would have to contend with my brother's need to play with the new toy he bought me. I patiently listened and waited as

Validation—Is It True What They Say?

my brother went through his favorite parts of the book. I knew he would have to tire of it eventually.

When I was finally able to retrieve my book from my brother, I found the section on Adam and Eve. This is when the slap in the face took place. The book stated Adam and Eve were angels from heaven. This book stated Heaven was a planet in another galaxy. I couldn't believe my eyes. It wasn't until my brother had gone, and I was home alone, that I read further.

Adam and Eve, the book related, were sent by God to mix with the humans and start a new race. I was in shock. I thought to myself, I am not alone. Someone else has received similar messages.

As I read more in the book, I found more validation and similarity. The book mentioned the "nameless ones" and the "I Am." I must state here, my writings were not exactly the same as *The Urantia Book*, but the similarity was unmistakable. This book went into great detail. My writings were few compared to the content of merely a small portion of this book. To date, I've read only a fraction of *The Urantia Book*.

This experience marked the beginning of my process of discovery. I had found interesting information in the *Bible*, but nothing so close to my actual writings. I knew there had to be some real meaning or reason for the messages I was receiving. I had a strong feeling there existed another book; something that could help me in some way with the writings. Little did I know I would find it in a few short weeks.

There was a book I saw in a catalog in November 1988. The title is what caught my eye. I felt very strongly I needed that book. I just knew it had something important for me. The book I'm referring to is *Secrets from Mount Shasta* by Earlyne Chaney. It seemed impossible to find, and so did the catalog I originally discovered it in.

In the beginning of January 1989, I was in a metaphysical bookstore in Sacramento. While sorting through the shelves I decided to ask the cashier if they had *Secrets of Mount Shasta*. She walked over to a shelf, pulled out a book and handed it to me. There it was, in my hand, *Secrets of Mount Shasta* by Earlyne Chaney. I could hardly wait to read it. If I thought *The Urantia Book* was a shocker, I had no idea what I was in for with this one.

When I thought this book had something in it for me, I was not mistaken. The book covered the author's experiences on Mount Shasta. It included her reason for going, and what happened while she was there.

The author and her husband started a foundation in the early 1950s named Astara. In the meetings or gatherings of the members, meditations and spirit communications took place. At that time (the early 1950s) she and her husband were told to go to Mount Shasta by "unseen teachers." They were to experience an initiation. The author was told verbally or through meditation that she must go. I was told through spirit writing.

Unlike me, the author and her husband did what they were told and went to the mountain. Earlyne Chaney wrote of a person she and her husband met on Mount Shasta, an ancient one if you will (I was told the ancient one would be waiting for me there). There was a gathering inside the mountain in which she and her husband had partaken. Information was given to them on the state of the earth and what could or would come about.

In my writings with Ankar and Ye, I was told I would know all very soon. It was communicated to me to go to the mountain, and all would make sense. I was also told that there were others who incarnated in this lifetime to help me. Earlyne Chaney was informed special souls would be incarnating. These special souls were to be the teachers and the messengers to the people. This book had a definite impact on me. The experiences of the author in the 1950s so closely paralleled mine in the late 1980s, it's dumbfounding.

Chapter 14

My Purpose—Who Am I, And What Am I Doing Here?

From the time I first started receiving the messages, Ankar and Ye repeatedly told me I am the "chosen one," and I am here to "save the world." I had been informed that I chose this, and that Ye and Ankar among others are here to help me on my way.

On January 8, 1989, Ankar wrote:

Angels of God are here for you, because you are a child... Children of God are always protected by angels of God.

Ankar also tried to warn me:

Angels can be good or bad, as can anyone else. There are good angels and there are bad angels, all are not the same.

Ankar proceeded to tell me I'd been here before. He also wrote:

> *All is what it should be at this time. You will see only what can be seen at this time.*

That makes sense. I suppose he was trying to tell me all things would be apparent in due time. He didn't hesitate to continue to tell me about the impending change. He wrote:

> *Go now and sleep. Soon you will awaken to a new life and a new world. This is the calm before the storm. In all the world, you Əfero, are the only one with the power and the knowledge to make the difference.*

That is certainly placing a lot on my shoulders, especially considering I felt I didn't know anything. Then Ankar added:

> *You can and you will make a change, that the candles of heaven will burn freely... Candles of heaven. All will make sense very soon.* (I hope it's real soon, because that did not succeed in making me feel less confused.)

Ankar had a way with words. He was always trying to reassure me about everything. He often told me how much he loved me. He always told me I had everything I needed. He wrote:

> *God is with you, as are we all. You can't let go of the purpose of being. Let me be your helper, Əfero. Let*

me help you through the dark time. You can lean on me, for I love you throughout the lifetime of eternities. You are to me, the light that burns the flame of love for all. Go to sleep now my special angel. Go to sleep and dream of happy... Cannot let go of you. Can't you see that all is for you? Say anything, and it shall be. All is at your command. All you must do is believe, and it is done. Thy will, get it? ...and it is done. Ankar

That was beautiful. It is the kind of thing we would want to hear from the person we are in love with. At least, I think it sounds pretty darn good. Naturally, I have an "entity" writing this to me, not some "in the flesh" kind of guy. Oh, well, at least I have someone saying nice things to me, even if he is other-dimensional.

Ankar and Ye once wrote that I emanated an energy that is detectable to those who are sensitive to it. They told me this would give me away. Then they told me I wasn't a normal human being. (That I believe!) Evidently, the reason I'm not a normal human being is because I am of the angels. I was a special child of God. (That wasn't exactly why I thought I wasn't normal, but it definitely sounds better than what had been in my mind.) Evidently, because of this difference, I was detectable to those "anglomen" who were sensitive to my energy. Basically, I was a dead giveaway. Apparently, that's the reason I need so much protection around me.

This information made me wonder. Ankar once told me to stop talking to anyone about my writings, for a while. He told me it was dangerous at that time. Ironically, my brother called me and told me the same thing. This happened within a few days of Ankar's warning. My brother told me not to send any of my writings through the mail, and not to show them to anyone I didn't know.

This was certainly a time of high intrigue. I thought to myself, what are you guys trying to do, make me nervous? Well, it was working. I was only unnerved for a couple of days, and then I didn't let it bother me. Of course, I didn't send any writing through the mail, or talk to any strangers about it. I decided, true or not, why take chances.

It's funny, as many times as Ankar and Ye (as well as all the other entities) have told me why I'm here, I still couldn't seem to get it through my head. I had this steadfast disbelief. I suppose the feeling foremost in my mind was that of unworthiness—that and wondering how the heck I got in this position. A person I'd met told me being a chosen one isn't all it's cracked up to be. Being chosen means one was volunteered.

My writings state I chose to be here. Perhaps I was among a group of volunteers, and from that group were selected "The Chosen." Who's to say? I know I

My Purpose—Who Am I, And What Am I Doing Here?

certainly have no other way of knowing for sure. All I have to go on is what has been written to me. I kept asking questions and they kept answering.

What is it that I must do?
You must go out among the people. You must give them all you can. This is your calling. Speak to them, tell them what you know. Tell them what you have learned. Share yourself with them. Your reward is, angel of God. You hold the keys. You will open the locked entry into the path of the God of truth and light. Go out among them. Show them the way, as they are lost lambs being led to slaughter. May you be a safe and protected angel of light. You are the light, you are the way.

Once, in the beginning of February 1989, I wrote to Ankar and Ye after a period of not writing.

We haven't communicated in a while. How are you?
All is well with us. It is you who needs to see yourself well. Ǝfero, you look as though you are slowly dying. Why? You must take care of yourself. You must take care of business and you must be ready. It, as you know, is approaching that time. All will be absolutely crystal clear soon, crystal clear.

Is this in my lifetime?

Yes Ðfero, you are the sign. You are the sign. There will be a dove as eyes will have never seen. This dove carries with it a sign, a message in the form of a letter from the All Father. We must make a place of safety. For those who believe will be safe from the change, and the effect it will have on those beings of flesh. Go out in the plane [sic] and tell them of this, as this change will begin soon, very soon. Be at peace all of you, for you are witness to the gift of God to the world. Take heed that no one can change the course of events to come. It has already begun. All will be a new earth. All will be good.

What is a safe place?
All will be crystal clear to you, Ðfero. All will be crystal clear very soon.

Are people going to die because of this change?
Yes, Ðfero, there will be many, but this is what must take place. All will be all right, because those who do leave this plane will be in the light and will be safe and secure. Fear not, Ðfero, the world will be a God-like planet again, and all can begin again. We must remember, we have a mission, and that is our purpose of being. This is Ankar and Ye.

It used to drive me crazy when they would tell me that, "All will be crystal clear." They

My Purpose—Who Am I, And What Am I Doing Here?

communicated it a lot! What exactly did they mean by "crystal clear"? I still don't know.

Chapter 15

The End Time, PTSD, and Spiritual Boot Camp

We are in the end time. Sounds pretty ghastly doesn't it? However horrible it may sound, that is what Ankar and Ye repeatedly told me. This is the end time, the second coming, the beginning of the end. Just what exactly does all this mean? I will attempt to share with you what I have come to understand.

It seems we came to a time where, many believed, the end of an era or age took place. On August 16, 1987, we experienced what was called the "Harmonic Convergence." Many believed this was the beginning of the "new age." I'm not exactly sure what was supposed to have happened after that day. Regardless, I'm sure for many people the days after, and the way life was lived, were unchanged. Not unlike the end of the Mayan calendar in December 2012. With all the anticipation and expectation, it ended up being rather underwhelming.

In 1987, I didn't even know what the Harmonic Convergence was. At that time, I heard in an interview that the changing of the age could take twenty years or so. It may have passed us by, seemingly unnoticed, or we are still in the slow process of transition from one age to the other. The Harmonic Convergence brought about no drastic changes (that I know of), and nothing occurred "all of a sudden;" however, eight months later I started receiving the messages from the angels. Ironically, approximately eight months before the Harmonic Convergence, a man now known as Ra Uru Hu, received messages from a "voice" while living on the island of Ibiza in Spain. The messages he received later became the very complex system known as Human Design.

Astrologically speaking, approximately every two thousand years marks the change of the sign of the age. As of the time of Jesus Christ, give or take a little, we have been in the age of Pisces. We are on the edge of the change into the Aquarian age. It could be that the "end time" means the end of the Piscean age.

Those who follow the Bible may view the end time differently. The end time, to many of Bible-believing people, is the Day of Judgment; the end of the world. I was taught in Catholic school; the Day of Judgment was the day all souls were divided between good and bad. They were then placed on their prospective sides of God. This separation determined those who were heaven bound, and those who were hell bound. Different belief systems have differing views on what the end times entail; however, going into those systems is beyond the purview of this book.

I asked Ankar and Ye to tell me more about the end times. They wrote, "Changes are actually occurring right now, so you will come to understand all of this soon, very soon." Well, I didn't understand, and I still questioned all of this. Ankar and Ye went on to write,

> *A new man has come into the picture. There will be social unrest. There will be many changes. There will be a life as not known before. There will be a life as you cannot dream. You will be one with the All, the All Father.*

I found this interesting, because in Nordic and Germanic mythology, the "All Father" is the god Odin, but I am pretty certain that is not who they meant. They also told me that they would be contacting me often during the time between my writings from 1988 and the "end times." They wrote, "Many times we will contact you between now and the last days. Be at ease. Stay close to the pen, as there will be much writing done." As time went by, I didn't stay close to the pen, because I was feeling the effects of knowing all of this. My life was changing. Ankar and Ye tried to cheer me up when they wrote,

All will see a new earth soon, and it will be an earth made new. It will be a second chance. It will be a sign. It will be a new saying for all to remember. The saying and the meaning will bring a light to the darkness. We are the light of the angels of God. We have come to awaken those who sleep. We are here to bring those out of the darkness. We are here to lighten the way. Go and be with God, all will be as it is to be. Once the light shines on this planet, all will no longer be as we have known.

Well, I was already feeling the "no longer be as we have known," and not in the way they intended. The fact that they insisted the change was coming was a little unsettling and I was becoming very unsettled. I felt an urgency about what was supposed to come, and the need to share the message. What I discovered when sharing this message was that many people didn't want to hear it, and Helen was one of them. Sometime during 1989 and 1990, Helen told me I was scaring her and she didn't want me talking about it around her. She also told me that I was scaring other people and I needed to chill out. She said I would scare away my clients at the psychic fairs I was working at the time. I have a feeling that to Helen, and perhaps others as well, I was sounding a bit like the grim reaper and the doomsday sayer. Yet, Ankar and Ye didn't lighten up. They told me,

We are on our way to the great purification. We are on the edge of the greatest change, to life, and this planet as we know it. Be not afraid, for as a chosen one you will be a leader of men. You will be the new light to the world. Among us there will be those who choose a different path, but that is up to them. We must stand steadfast and continue on. For this is the source of the new life for all who wish to partake of it.

Quite frankly, I was trying to escape the writings and the emotional trouble I started to experience. My experiences were affecting me, and as a result, my relationships, which led to a very painful breakup. Within a day of the breakup, I began having severe anxiety and panic attacks. It got to the point I was in muscle spasms on the floor, stuck in the fetal position, and I could not straighten up. Those spasms lasted for hours. I couldn't eat and could barely drink.

I was alone at home, and the only person I knew in the city I was living in at the time was my roommate. She happened to be away from home for a week where there was no phone access. I had no choice but to call my newly ex-boyfriend for help. He was not happy, to say the least. However, he did help me get a plane ticket to Arizona to stay with my mother, who was a nurse. I was fortunate to get into therapy right away with my presenting symptoms of anxiety disorder and panic disorder. An additional strange symptom developed, I could no longer perceive color in my vision. Everything was in shades of gray.

I was promptly diagnosed with PTSD and told it would take about ten years for me to feel normal again. That was unacceptable to me. I didn't want to believe it. I couldn't believe it, because if I did, it would leave me with a feeling of hopelessness and powerlessness. Fortunately, no matter how difficult, I was completely dedicated to my healing and went to therapy every day. I refused all allopathic medications, feeling they would slow my healing progress. I chose herbs and homeopathic remedies.

Quite frankly, I simply toughed it out. And, it was tough. I began to wonder if this was my own personal "end time"? During the toughest time, I sank into my lowest of lows, contemplating suicide (because no one should have to live that way for any length of time, much less ten years). Instead, I kept myself looking up with the firm belief, if not a firm knowing, that I would beat this. I had come to refer to that time as "Spiritual Boot Camp."

Some people would say to me, "Ask the angels for help." I couldn't. What was clear to me was that this was my "officer's training." We have to learn to be independent thinkers. Certainly, we may need help until we get our wings strong (no pun intended . . . sort of), but I knew what was necessary for me was to build my own strength in trusting my judgement and ability to discern. And, as providence would have it, Ankar and Ye had stepped back. Their presence was not easily discernable. I knew they would still come if I needed them, but they were distanced.

I had to learn to be a leader, if not for others, then at the very least for myself. One of my tests of personal leadership was taking control of the form of treatments that would be used for my healing. Several therapists refused to work with me if I wasn't on medication, so I continued to search for those who would. Ironically, the person who I ended up working with had walked into my life as one of my new astrology clients. After her session, we chatted. When she found out about my PTSD, she offered to work with me. I accepted. She was a gift. Using her alternative methods and modalities, I was symptom free within seven months. The color also returned to my vision. I may have passed the test and graduated from the angels' officer's training, but was I ready to re-engage with the writings? I chose to start college instead. Yet, even that wasn't an escape from the messages.

On my first day, in my Native American Myth and Oral Tradition class (I mentioned this class very briefly in the "The New Race" chapter), I discovered the teacher was a Native American of the Wintun tribe. Guess where the Wintun tribe live—the base of Mount Shasta, of course. After introducing himself to the class, he proceeded to talk about the Lemurians in the mountain (face palm!). After I lifted my jaw off the top of my desk, I realized, there truly was no escape from this.

Chapter 16

What is to Come

From the writings we are told the world is not as it seems. We are told the change is coming soon. My main angels said the change is coming very soon. Other angels, who popped in every now and then, said there will be time between now and the "change." Regardless of the timing, the angels were ringing out the news that events are going to occur.

Great things are about to take place, great things. Can you be ready for the excitement? We are here for you. We are always here for you. Mend your ways, for much is at hand. The world will never be the same. We will give time to those who choose to go with us. We will give you time to get what you need. All will be anew. We will revel in the glory. Entities, there is much to do. The time is at hand. We will be in the light of God once again. We will be illumined by the almighty. Archangel Michael and Archangel Aniel

This rings of the "rapture," which is part of the belief system of many Christian denominations. At the time this message came to me, I had never heard of the rapture. Similar to the Christian rapture, there is a large group of people in the world who believe that there will be a mass "ascension," and that they are experiencing physiological changes in preparation for, or as a result of, the changes associated with the ascension. There are also some UFOlogy folks who believe that a giant ship is coming to take people off the planet during the dire earth changes. It is my understanding, in all of these scenarios, whoever is left behind will experience physical death or remain in their lower density dimension.

As I wrote before, I used to be quite afraid of death. This fear was especially impactful when I watched my father dying. He was so afraid to die, it broke my heart and made me feel completely powerless to help him. Through the years, since the angels first started writing to me, I have studied a variety of literature on life, death, and life after death. In addition, I have had my own personal experiences in research regarding survival of consciousness. From all of this, I have come to my own sense of peace about death.

What is to Come

My own knowingness tells me that what Ye and Ankar (and all the other angels, for that matter) were telling me may be true, or at least a good deal of it. This is because I am not the only person who has received these messages. That does make a difference, if not to the veracity of the messages, then to the messages not being the questionable experience of only one person. It must mean those of us who have received similar messages have a link to the universal energies and/or the cosmic forces of some kind. Perhaps even intelligence from another planet and/or dimension is communicating to those sensitive to their "voices." The messages may even be from entities on our own planet, only existing on another dimension.

Irrespective of their origin, these messengers have the same concerns. They are trying to help us and warn us of the coming change, so we can prepare ourselves. Those of us who are in tune to their messages will benefit. There are those who are not meant to move with the shift. According to the messages I received from the angels, that is as it should be. Ankar and Ye were quite happy about what was to come. They wrote,

> *There will come to pass, a new day will dawn, upon a new time, a new life, a new world, a new man. Among you will again walk the giants, the angels, the gods. We will begin a new race again, Əfero, as it was in days past. Lemuria will be again reborn, and a*

> *new life for all will be. A new life for all who wish it so.*

I know, regardless of what is to come or what is not to come, in each moment of our lives we are in control of so much. We can influence the outcome of the social consciousness. Our thoughts are so powerful. We can raise our own vibrations by changing the way we look at things, our perceptions, our feelings, and our reactions. If we come from a point of love and can be without judgment, we can change our lives, and at the same time influence the people and the world around us. It is up to each of us. Ankar and Ye wrote,

> *The after time* [the end of the end time?] *is close at hand. The after time will bring new life for all who choose to remain. We will see a new world. We will see Eden again. We must tend to our garden if we want it to remain alive and glowing. We must be aware of its needs. We must protect it from those things that will harm it. We need to know we have a home to which we may return. We want to keep it safe.*

Ankar went on to write,

> *Man and the animals will experience great change. All will be different soon. There will be those among you who will not accept these things that are written, but that is as it should be. Some of you are not meant*

to go with the others. Be at our side dear ones, for a great new world awaits us all.

This sentiment was reiterated several times during the time of my main writings. The concern for the planet was paramount. An entity that identified itself as Archangel Aniel, wrote,

Let it be said that the voice in the silence has spoken. Let it be written that the sign of the time and the sign of the signal has come. We are now facing a devastating problem. The accidents that are taking place around the globe, are triggering a chain reaction that cannot be reversed. The destruction from the failings of man have crippled our fragile ecosystem. Soon there will be a great panic among the people as the fish will wash up from the sea. They carry their disease to those who starve enough to consume them. Soon the stench of those decaying remains will be the cause for nausea around the world. The poison is spreading. The poison is spreading.

Ankar and Ye wrote,

We worry about those things that are going to end soon. We need to concern ourselves with what is happening to the world, to the people, to the animals. We need to address the issues that affect the masses. We are only here for a short time, and all the while those who can do something don't. Those who stand

> *by and watch the destruction are just as guilty as those who do it. We are in the process of slowly creating another wasteland.*

Too many of us in the Western world have become so "addicted" to the material things and comforts of life and developed a throwaway mentality (which is rapidly resulting in a negative impact on this planet and its inhabitants). I feel, because of this attitude, sometimes we are slow to move or change. For far too many people, this complacency is a status quo state of being. The "neetnas" or the "anglomen" won't need to come again to try and destroy the planet, people will be doing the job themselves. When something beyond our control happens, and our life is directly affected, our values suddenly shift. It is this value shift that is needed for all of us to open our eyes and change our ways. I hope the shift in values occurs before the problems truly are irreversible.

The angels indicated that the end time is coming "soon, very soon." Reflecting on this time factor, I have to ask, what the heck is "soon" to an angel? Here is a little piece that I think illustrates this notion. I do not know the author, perhaps it's from an old parable. It goes like this:

A man asked God, "What's a million years to you?"

God said, "A second."

What is to Come

Then the man asked God, "What's a million dollars to you?"

God said, "A penny."

Then the man asked God, "Will you give me a penny?"

God said, "Yes, in a second."

I leave you now, to end this here, but before I go, I ask you, what would you do if you received these messages? Who (or what) do you think the angels are? I'd love to hear your thoughts about the writings. Feel free to follow me on Facebook:

https://www.facebook.com/DrIreneBlinston

About the Author

Dr. Irene Blinston has seen and experienced "some weird things" in her life. The events shared in this book are among the many unexplained, little understood, and mysterious phenomena Dr. Blinston experienced beginning in her childhood and continuing into adulthood. These experiences include a religious apparition, lucid and repeating dreams, psychic phenomena, odd electrical and magnetic phenomena involving her body, out of body experiences (OBEs), spontaneous weeping, the scent of sanctity, UFO sightings, seeing Big Foot, and more. These experiences are what led Dr. Blinston to pursue her Ph.D. in transpersonal psychology, which included the study of psychic phenomena, survival of consciousness after death, encounter experiences, mystical experiences, altered states of consciousness, and more. Dr. Blinston knows that by revealing our experiences we risk being called crazy, or worse. But, it is this lack of exposure that keeps these aspects of our human potential misunderstood, understudied, and sometimes labeled as pathology.

Made in the USA
Lexington, KY
22 December 2018